What the Experts Say about Bullies to Buddies

Paul Reddick, Chairman, American Sportsmanship Association

The American Sportsmanship Association officially endorses Izzy Kalman and his techniques.

If you are serious about putting a stop to bullying and teasing you must use Izzy Kalman's techniques. I have spoken to hundreds of groups about bullying and teasing and never saw the results that I have after applying Izzy's strategies. I have seen every other program designed to stop this problem, but Izzy's is the only one that works! Read his books, buy his tapes, hire him to speak, and you will have results.

Dr. Bernie Stein, President of the International School Psychology Association, 1999-2001

This book is an important contribution that conveys a clear message to children, parents and teachers: there is a way out; something can be done to stop the suffering of victims. It is an easy to read and practical guide on how to break behavior patterns seemingly deeply entrenched, telling victims they need not remain in this role.

The book also deals with bullying at home: – parents who are violent toward their children and siblings fighting with each other. Families can learn how to create a more harmonious life for themselves and a healthier environment for their children, preventing the recurrent pattern of children who are victims of violence becoming violent when they grow up.

Samuel Albert, PhD, Psychologist

Mr. Kalman builds upon a common sense but not-so-obvious truth about the evolution of human anger to explain why bullying occurs, how children, parents and schools tend to mishandle this problem, and how it can be eliminated. His professional experience with children over many years is evident throughout. Although written for children and adolescents, this book should be read by all parents as well for the insights it offers into everyday anger and the ways we needlessly make ourselves miserable. Readers will be surprised at times by the advice in this sometimes unconventional but always highly readable book. So far as I know, there is no other approach like it. Highly recommended.

Steven Sussman, PhD, Director, Child & Teen Success Centers

Izzy's book transcends typical therapy books. He utilizes wisdom of the ages to explain common psychological phenomena and empowers all of us with his unique teachings. I recommend this book to anyone has an open mind and is looking for real techniques to help themselves and others.

George Anthony, Director, Peace Dynamics Consultants

I have found Izzy Kalman's strategies in combating teasing/bullying to be an effective deterrent. What Izzy offers are skills to effectively communicate to an adversary that I will not allow your words or actions to hurt me. That is a gift many children as well as parents search for.

Newton Hightower, LMSW-ACP, Director of The Center for Anger Resolution, Inc.
Author of ANGER BUSTING 101: New ABC's for Angry Men and The Women Who Love Them

This book would have kept me out of the principal's office during grade school. Instead, I was taught to fight back. The problem is that if I won the fight, then I would be in trouble and have someone else to fight the next day. Suddenly, people thought I was the bully.

This is a fantastic book with clear instructions, illustrations and short tests to make sure we get the ideas!

I agree 100% with his approach of teaching kids new phrases to say. These are the same phrases I teach angry men, such as, "You are right!" There is NO WAY to have an argument if you are agreeing with the other person. Those three words prevent all arguments at 10 years of age or 110.

This is the perfect book for all of us 10 years old and up — parents and kids — victims or bullies!

Bullies to Buddies

How to Turn Your Enemies into Friends

Izzy Kalman

BULLIES TO BUDDIES
How to Turn Your Enemies into Friends

Izzy Kalman, MS, NCSP

Copyright ©2005 by Izzy Kalman

The Wisdom Pages
65 Fraser St.
Staten Island, NY 10314

Publisher's Cataloging-in-Publication
(Provided by Quality Books, Inc.)
Kalman, Izzy.
Bullies to buddies: how to turn your enemies into friends / Izzy Kalman.
p.   cm.
SUMMARY: Suggests strategies for kids to stop being teased and bullied, and shows how to improve relationships with peers, siblings, parents, and teachers.
Audience: Grades 6-12.
LCCN 2003100319
ISBN 0-9706482-1-9

1.   Social interaction—Juvenile literature.
2.   Problem solving—Juvenile literature.
3.   Bullying—Prevention—Juvenile literature.
4.   Teasing—Prevention—Juvenile literature.

[1. Interpersonal relations. 2. Teasing. 3. Bullying. 4. Conduct of life.] I. Title.

HQ784.S56K35 2004   302.3
                           QBI04-810

The advice in this book is based on the author's two decades of experience helping victims of teasing and bullying. It is not intended as a substitute for professional counseling and the publisher makes no claims for its effectiveness. If problems persist, the help of a competent professional should be sought.

Cover Design by Lola Kalman
Ceramic Cover Art by Jamey Breinberg
Book Design and Production by Danny Cohen

For more information, visit **www.Bullies2Buddies.com.**

This book is available at quantity discounts for bulk purchases. For information, call 1-866-983-1333.

Acknowledgements

I am a very lucky person. I don't know how many people can say they lead as satisfying a life as I do. It is all due to luck. If there is a Higher Power that has been sending luck my way, then my first thanks go to Him/Her/It/Them.

There are many mortals who deserve my deepest thanks for having made this book possible. First on the list are my family members. My beloved wife, Miri, has suffered me and encouraged me for twenty-two years. Our children, Lola, Yannai, and Ayala have permitted me to be a neglectful father while I attend to my projects, and have served as unwitting guinea pigs in many of my psychological experiments. My parents, Brenda and Michael (may he rest in peace), have made it all possible, and my sister, Ruth Grafstein, and her wonderful family have always stood behind me.

About eighteen years ago, a teenaged student once asked me, "What should you do when someone calls you names?" I didn't know it at the time, but that was probably the most fateful question I ever received. The answer to that question started me on my journey of helping victims of teasing and bullying. I don't remember the boy's name, but I sure am grateful to him. The course of my life might have been completely different if not for him. And I never would have written this book.

I'd like to thank the school principals who have given me the opportunity to practice and develop my techniques in their schools. Most particularly, my thanks to Paul Choset and Judy Horowitz, the principals of P.S. 54 and P.S. 26 respectively, in Staten Island, New York. May you both enjoy your retirements. My fourteen years with the New York City Board of Education would not have been the same without the support and camaraderie of my School Based Support Team colleagues, Bonnie Brienberg, Ed Schwarz, and Lisa Volpe.

I have been incredibly fortunate to have clinical supervisors who did much more than make sure I did my job. My first supervisor was Bernie Stein. Bernie ran the school psychology clinic in Ashkelon, Israel, and it was the best learning environment anyone could hope for. He provided us with an endless stream of interesting (and often unconventional) lecturers to expand our conceptions of what therapy could be. I can't overstate how lucky I am to have worked under the guidance of someone who so strongly encouraged experimentation on the job. Bernie went on to become chief school psychologist of Israel and served as President of the International School Psychology Association. Later, luck delivered Dr. Rachel Deouell to me.

As my supervisor in private practice, she helped me discover quick ways of helping people. Luck followed me when I moved back to the United States and sent me to Dr. Allan Pincus, supervisor of school psychologists in Staten Island. Allan, I thank you for encouraging my work on teasing and bullying and for repeatedly getting me out of hot water.

A few years ago, luck took the form of Dr. Steve Sussman, director of the Child and Teen Success Centers of New York and New Jersey. I could write a book on how important he has been to me personally and professionally. I don't know if there is anyone who uses humor in therapy more effectively than he does. Thanks, Steve, for introducing me to John Jones, director of Cross Country University. And thanks, John, for sending me around the country teaching my methods to other professionals.

Lastly, I'd like to thank several people who have helped me on this book. Monica Rosenberg not only is a great editor, she practically taught me how to write. Judith Szenes, thanks for your artistic support and for introducing Monica to me. Our good family friend, Jamey Breinberg (son of Bonnie mentioned above), is the mad ceramics genius who made the faces on the book cover and has argued with me about bullying for years. I am lucky to have a funny and artistic daughter, Lola, who created the humorous illustrations in the book and arranged the book cover. Lola and my son, Yannai, both did valuable reviews of the manuscript. Special thanks also to Dr. Sam Albert for your extremely thorough review. And thanks, Danny Cohen, for your typesetting talents.

There are many other people who deserve my thanks no less than those I have mentioned. Please forgive me for leaving your name out. This is a short book and I don't want to turn it into a long one.

This book is dedicated to you.

Table of Contents

Section Three: Some Good Advice   **55**

Section Four: Specific Situations   **71**

Introductory Notes for Parents and Teachers

The rash of tragic school shootings, epitomized by Columbine, shocked the modern world. It emerged that these horrific incidents were committed almost exclusively by victims of teasing and bullying. In response, parents, educators, and mental health professionals have been advocating for the right of children to go to school without fear of bullies. Since then, schools nationwide have been adopting anti-bullying programs and regulations.

Despite their wonderful intentions, many of these anti-bullying measures are having only minor success in reducing the incidence of bullying in schools. In fact, many educators have informed me that bullying in their schools has *increased* since implementing anti-bullying programs.

There are reasons for the limited success of anti-bullying programs:

1. When experts tell students how terrible it is to tease and bully other kids and that these behaviors shouldn't be tolerated, it may get some kids to be more considerate towards others. However, this message is a double-edged sword. It also gives students the message that they *should* get upset when they are on the receiving end of teasing and bullying. Thus, when they are picked on, instead of shrugging it off – which is the smart thing to do, they are more likely to think, *"How dare they treat me that way!"* Getting upset by bullying has the unintended effect of perpetuating bullying.

2. Students are being instructed that "telling is not tattling." They are being encouraged, and in some schools even forced, to tell whenever anyone bothers them or when they witness others being picked on. Informing the authorities on people is about the best legal way to get them to hate you and to want revenge against you. If you are not sure of this, try this simple experiment: The next time your neighbors do something you don't like, call the police on them.

3. School personnel are being required to intervene when kids quarrel. Unfortunately, this almost always escalates hostilities. In fact, most of the bickering and fighting that goes on between kids is actually caused unwittingly by the attempts of adults to make kids get along. Thus, educators are being required to do the very thing that makes kids fight.

While adults are fighting for the right of kids to be free of teasing and bullying, few realize that this right has existed all along. It is guaranteed by the US Constitution, in the First Amendment of The Bill of Rights. It is called "Freedom of Speech." Freedom of speech is actually the Constitutional version of the age-old slogan, "Sticks and stones may break my bones but words will never harm me." About ninety percent of the incidents we call bullying are actually name-calling, and even most physical fights begin with verbal insults. Kids call each other bad names, they get angry, they threaten each other, and before you know it fists are flying. When kids know how to practice freedom of speech – lettings others say what they want without getting angry or trying to stop them – they don't become victims of relentless teasing and bullying. Unfortunately, instead of promoting freedom of speech, the anti-bully movement is suppressing it. In our effort to protect our kids from aggression, we are depriving them of the solution to aggression.

The solution to aggression is also embodied by the Golden Rule. This requires "treating others the way you want to be treated." In other words, you are to treat others like friends even when they are treating you like an enemy. By doing so, you turn your enemies into friends. Unfortunately, the anti-bullying programs violate the Golden Rule. They require people to be even meaner to bullies than the bullies are to their victims. You're not sure about this? I'll give you the following choice. Let's say we work together and I don't like something you did. In response I will either (a) call you an idiot (or the insult of your choice) a thousand times, or (b) get you in trouble with your boss. Which would you prefer? You almost certainly would choose (a), because getting you in trouble with your boss is a much worse thing for me to do to you than insulting you. Yet we are suspending kids from school and sometimes even expelling them for the terrible "crime" of name-calling.

Two ways of helping victims
If you are a victim of bullying, there are two basic ways to solve your problem. One way is by forcing everyone in the world to stop bullying, and then you will be free of bullying. The other way is by teaching you how to stop being a victim.

However, even the best-researched anti-bullying programs claim only a 50% reduction in bullying. If your happiness depends upon the success of the campaign against bullies, you will spend the rest of your life in misery.

On the other hand, if you know how to handle bullying, you don't have to wait for the world to change. Your problem is solved in no time.

And that is the purpose of this book. It solves the problem of victims in the most efficient way possible: by teaching them how to turn their bullies into buddies. The beautiful thing about this is that it creates a win/win situation. When victims stop being victims, bullies stop being bullies. And the adults win, too, because they have better things to do with their time than mediate endless conflicts between children.

The ideas in this book may seem radical because they are contrary to almost everything that is being said and done today about bullying. But the truth is that there is absolutely nothing new in this book. My teachings are totally consistent with the wisdom of the ages. Whether your spiritual hero is Jesus, Moses, Mohammed, the Buddha, Confucius, Gandhi, the Founding Fathers, or Martin Luther King, Jr., you should love what this book does for your children and students.

Thank you for giving this approach a try.

Best wishes,

Izzy Kalman

Section One: Understanding Life

The Animal Within

Do you wonder how kids can be so cruel to you? Does it seem as if they're acting like animals?

Well, you are right. They *are* acting like animals. Because they *are* animals. And so are you. We all are. Sure, we may have eternal souls that put us on a higher spiritual level than other animals. We have brains that enable us to accomplish things no other animal can. But as long as we are alive, we never stop being animals.

We are animals?

Years ago, I read books by world-famous zoologist and writer, Desmond Morris. Desmond Morris is an expert in animals. Thanks to his extensive knowledge, he was able to demonstrate that much of human behavior is actually animal behavior. He also showed that many of the problems people have today are the same as those that animals develop when they live in zoos rather than in their natural environment.

Thinking about human beings the way Desmond Morris does, I found ways to help people solve many of their problems, especially with aggression and violence. I have taught thousands of people how to get others to treat them better, and that's what I will teach you. The lessons won't be hard to understand and they won't require much effort.

If people are picking on you and making you miserable — and you can't stop them no matter how hard you try — it is because the animal part of us is acting according to rules that no longer help us in our normal lives. Animals are born with a full set of instincts and reactions that they need to survive. And so are we. Until several thousand years ago, when humans became civilized, we lived in nature like all animals. Our brains haven't changed much and are still designed for life in nature. Unfortunately, some of the basic rules for success in civilization are very different from those in nature. Our inborn behaviors, instead of helping us succeed, make us fail.

I will teach you how the rules have changed and how to succeed according to the new rules. Fortunately, succeeding in civilization is much easier than succeeding in nature. Today everyone can be a winner, including you.

Who Can Help You

Jordan came to my office asking for help. He had been teased and bullied by kids in school every day, and he couldn't stand it anymore. I discussed his situation with Principal Hawthorne. She decided we should call an assembly since this was a common problem in the school.

With 1,200 students facing me in the large school auditorium, I described how terrible it is to be mean to other kids. I explained that teasing hurts kids' feelings and that bullying makes them scared. I told them they should never tease or bully anyone and that they should not tolerate anyone who does. Whenever they see anyone picking on another student, they should immediately step in to stop the bully or get an adult to help.

One month later, Jordan returned to my office to thank me. He said everyone had become nice to him. Principal Hawthorne called to tell me the assembly was a huge success and had convinced all the students it was wrong to tease and bully. There was peace among the students. Teachers were able to spend all their time teaching instead of trying to stop kids from fighting.

Are you thinking this story sounds too good to be true? Well, you are right! It is a fairy tale. For thousands of years adults have been teaching kids to be nice to each other and punishing them for being cruel. And for thousands of years kids have continued to be cruel anyway. When teachers try to stop kids from bullying, they usually find themselves running a court trial, with both kids angrily arguing they were the victim and the other one the bully. The one who gets blamed and punished can't wait for the next opportunity to get even.

Why didn't I call in sick today?

I'm sorry to bring you the bad news: If you are waiting for adults around you to make kids stop bullying you, you may find yourself suffering for the rest of your life. Bullying doesn't only happen to kids in school. It goes on between adults at work. It happens among drivers on the road. The worst bullying of all actually takes place within families. Children and parents bully each other. Brothers and sisters bully each other. Many husbands and wives bully each other, too. So if you're looking forward to a bully-free life when you finish school, you are setting yourself up for disappointment.

No, I can't make the bullies of the world leave you alone, and neither can your parents, teachers, principal, friends or even the police.

The good news: Someone does have the power to make everyone stop tormenting you. That person is *you*.

Does this thought scare you? Don't worry. It won't be hard to do. I will show you how easy it is to make people stop picking on you and get them to like you and respect you more. Best of all, you will be able to stop bullies without anyone else's help and without getting anyone in trouble. All by yourself, you will be able to turn your bullies into buddies, and it will be easier than you thought possible. The rules you learn in this book will help you get along with others for the rest of your life.

The Misery of Being a Victim

Have you had about as much as you can take of kids picking on you? Whether it's the whole class or just one kid, teasing and bullying can make your life miserable.

Do other kids treat you like dirt? Do they call you ugly or stupid or gay? Do they make fun of your mother or your religion or the color of your skin? Do they spread mean rumors about you? Do they push you and hit you? Do they threaten to beat you up if you don't do what they want? Are the popular kids too embarrassed to even speak to you?

Have you tried everything to stop these kids? Calling them names back? Hitting them? Have you tried ignoring them, only to find the situation gets worse? Have you told on them to your teachers and principal? And are you the one who usually gets in trouble even though they started with you?

Has school become a nightmare? Do you hate going because you know you'll be abused some more? Do you sit in class, nervously wondering when the next insult will be hurled at you? Are you afraid to answer questions out loud because kids may laugh at you? Instead of paying attention to your classwork, do you spend time thinking up clever ways to respond to your bullies? And do you find that no matter how you respond, you end up looking and feeling bad?

Are you afraid to hang out in your own neighborhood because mean kids torment, threaten or hit you?

Do you feel like a pressure cooker, so filled with anger that you are ready to explode? Do you dream about ways to get revenge against your bullies? Even worse, do you ever think about ending your life so that you won't have to be miserable any longer?

You may feel totally alone. It may seem like you are the only one who suffers from this terrible problem. But you're not. Being teased and bullied is one of the most common problems in the world. In almost every classroom one or two kids get teased and bullied every day. Yes, there are millions and millions of kids who suffer just like you. And they all hate it.

If I could solve my bully problem, so can you.

But don't despair. No matter how short or tall or round you are, what race or religion you belong to, what clothes you wear, whether you have glasses or a big nose or ears that could be airplane wings, no one will continue picking on you after you learn the secrets in this book.

Follow these simple instructions and you will begin defeating your bullies right away. Within a week, hardly anyone will bother you, and if they try, they'll feel like losers and quickly stop. Since you won't be getting anyone in trouble, you won't have to worry that they'll want revenge. When you turn bullies into buddies, the fear of going to school or hanging out in the neighborhood will be over for good. You will be able to go almost anywhere without being afraid.

Other good things will start happening when you stop being a victim. Life will be brighter, and you will feel calmer, happier and more confident than you have in a long time. Your sense of humor will improve and being around other people will be more fun. Your brothers and sisters will stop fighting with you and will like you better. And your parents will like you better, too.

A Little Story

Billy goes for a walk and comes across an old house. In front of it stands a boy surrounded by dozens of pigeons. The boy is throwing pieces of bread on the sidewalk.

"What are you doing?" Billy asks the boy.

"I'm making the pigeons go away," the boy answers.

"What do you mean, you're making them go away?" Billy asks.

"Every morning, these birds come to our house. They are a terrible nuisance. The noise is unbearable, and the poop they leave all over the sidewalk is disgusting."

"So why are you throwing them bread?" Billy asks.

"The only way to get rid of them is to throw them bread. As soon as the last crumb is finished, they suddenly can't stand being here. They all fly away and we don't see them again for a whole day!"

What does this story have to do with being teased and bullied? Lots! Have patience and you'll soon understand.

Why You Are Picked On

Why do some kids become the regular victims of bullies? There is only one reason, and it's always the same. The most important step in making the bullying stop is understanding why you are picked on in the first place.

Maria suffers because kids call her four-eyes. She believes they taunt her because she wears glasses. But Maria is wrong. Sure, she wears glasses, but that's not why she is teased.

Serge is mad because he gets pushed every day on line in school. He thinks the kids do it because they hate him. But Serge is wrong. Maybe some kids hate him, but that's not why they push him.

Josh goes crazy when his classmates call him gay. It makes no sense to him because he likes girls. He thinks that maybe they do it because he's into art and doesn't care much about sports. But Josh is wrong. He may be artistic and unathletic, but that's not why the kids call him gay.

Aaliyah is miserable because kids spread rumors that she is stupid and gets lousy grades. She does great in school and aces all her tests. Aaliyah believes the kids are spreading rumors because they are jealous of her. But she's wrong. Maybe the other kids wish they had her good grades, but that's not why they are talking about her.

Thomas often cries because kids in school call him retarded. He thinks they are cruel to him because he is dyslexic and in a Special Ed class. But Thomas is wrong. He has trouble learning how to read, but that is not why kids call him retarded.

There is only one reason these kids are being picked on, but none of them can see it. It's also the reason you are picked on, but you can't see it either.

This is what you do see. First, the kids bully you. Then you get mad and try to make them stop. It seems like the kids start the bullying and you are trying to make it stop. But the truth is the other way around. The real reason they bully you is *because* you get mad and try to stop them. Without realizing it, you are actually *making* them bully you.

"What do you mean, I am making them bully me!" You may be thinking, *"That doesn't make any sense! I'm not making them bully me. I'm only trying to make them stop!"*

But, believe it or not, you *are* making them bully you. You just can't see it because the bullying happens first and your efforts to stop the bullying come afterwards. We are used to thinking that the first event in time causes the second event. And here I am, telling you that the second event — your attempt to stop the bullying — actually caused the bullying to happen. This sounds crazy because the bullying happened first!

But it's not crazy. When you get mad at kids who call you names or push you, how do they feel? Are they sad about what they did? They sure aren't. If they felt bad about bothering you, they wouldn't do it. When they bother you and you get mad, they love it. They feel great! They can't get enough of it. You feel lousy, and the angrier you get, the more fun they have and the better they feel.

Whatever you do to stop the bullying only makes the bullies feel more powerful. They're thinking inside, *"Go ahead, try to stop me. You can't do it no matter how hard you try!"* Even if you hide your feelings, it's probably not working. Feelings are hard to hide for long. Chances are, the bullies know you are upset from the look on your face and the way you behave, and this makes them feel good.

...not listening...
not listening...not
listening...

You see, they are not calling you "fatso" because you are fat, or "four-eyes" because you wear glasses. They really don't care about how you look. All they really care about is having fun. We all like to have fun, and one great way to have fun is to drive someone else crazy.

Your tormentors have discovered they can tease you and make you mad. They look for your weak spots, the things you are really embarrassed about and don't want anyone to notice.

The things you are most sensitive about usually have some truth to them. For instance, you are short and the kids discover you can't stand it when they call you "midget." Or you wear glasses, and it bugs you to be called "four-eyes." Or your mother is overweight, and you go totally bonkers when they make "fat" jokes about her.

Hmmm, whaddya know?
I really *do* have bad breath...
Could it be...*cigarettes?*

It probably wouldn't bother you if they said things that have nothing to do with the truth. For instance, if they said, "Your camel has bad breath," you'd just think, *"What a dumb thing to say. I don't even have a camel."*

But it really doesn't matter if the things they say are true. All that matters is that it bothers you. If you are beautiful but get mad when they call you "ugly," they will keep calling you "ugly." If you are thin and you get upset when they call you "fatso," they will keep calling you "fatso." Whatever succeeds in annoying you is exactly what they are going to do again and again.

If words don't bother you but kids discover you can't stand it when they put their hands on you, then pushing or hitting becomes a great way to defeat you. When you get mad, they have fun and want to do it again. And if you get in trouble because the teacher catches you hitting them back, they have even more fun!

The only thing that matters to them is being able to upset you. This gives them pleasure, so it goes on and on, day after day after day, like a train going endlessly around a track. The kids pick on you, you get mad, and they have fun. They pick on you, you get mad, and they have fun.

The anger you feel when you are bullied is like the bread fed to those pigeons. You are inspiring your bullies with crumbs of anger, thinking your anger is going to make them leave you alone. But your anger is exactly what keeps the bullies coming back day after day. They look forward to it! You make them so happy when you get angry that they *never* want to stop bullying you.

Yes, believe it or not, you have been rewarding your bullies for making fun of you. They have so much fun when they torment you that they want to do it as much as possible.

Taking Responsibility

It may sound like I'm blaming you for being bullied. I'm not. You had no way of knowing what was really going on. The smartest kids make the same mistake. So do adults. The same thing can go on in any relationship. Whether it's parents and children, husbands and wives, or brothers and sisters always arguing and fighting with each other, they are all making the same mistake. They don't realize that by getting mad they are practically *forcing* the other person to treat them in a way they can't stand. So, don't blame yourself. It's not your fault.

Don't blame anyone else, either. The only way you can improve your life is by taking responsibility and deciding to do something that will solve your problem. Once you can say to yourself, *"I understand how I've been causing my suffering,"* you can begin taking control of your life and start feeling much, much better.

Remember, you are not blaming yourself. You are taking responsibility. Blaming won't get you anywhere, but taking responsibility will.

The Verbal Bullying Experiment

I want to tell you about a game I have played with thousands of people of all ages and backgrounds. For me, it has been like a scientific experiment that reveals important truths about human nature. I would like you to play this game with a few friends or relatives for two reasons: 1) It will give you terrific practice in stopping bullies; 2) It will help you understand secrets of human nature. (You may even want to turn this into a science experiment for school.)

Step 1: Tell your subject:

"I am going to play a game with you. Your job is to insult me and my job is to make you stop. Don't worry about really hurting my feelings. It's just a game and I want you to try your hardest to win."

(You must *really* be ready to hear their insults without getting upset.)

When the subjects insult you, act mad and yell at them to stop. Make your face turn red with anger and act aggravated as you scream things like: "Shut up!" "You can't talk to me like that!" "Show me respect!" Or "If you don't shut your mouth, you're really going to be sorry!"

Do you think your response will make your subjects stop? No way. They will smile and laugh and insult you even more. The angrier you become, the more they will enjoy insulting you. When your head is splitting and you can't go on any longer, say "I give up. You win."

Step 2: Say to your subject:

"We're going to play the game one more time. Your job is to insult me and my job is to make you stop."

This time, instead of getting mad and trying to make them stop, calmly listen and remain unaffected by anything they say. Let them know they can insult you all they want. Do you know what will happen? They will quickly become frustrated and give up.

You should discover that almost everyone responds the same way. No matter how kind or gentle the people may be, they have fun when you get angry and feel stupid when you don't.

It's human nature to enjoy driving people crazy. If I had the chance to play the game with you, I guarantee that you, too, would enjoy it when I get mad and feel foolish when I don't. It is not only bullies that enjoy upsetting people. We all do.

The Physical Bullying Experiment

Here is another experiment I want you to try. This one explores situations where kids try to upset you not only with words but by pushing or hitting you. Be careful not to change the order of the two steps.

Step 1: Ask a friend or family member to stand next to you. Then say, "Give me a push." After they push you, do absolutely nothing but go back and stand next to them. They will probably stand there, a bit confused. They may give you another little push, but probably do nothing after that.

Step 2: After waiting several seconds, say again, "Give me a push." This time when they push you, push back and yell, "Stop pushing me!" They will probably smile or laugh and immediately push you even harder.

This experiment shows that if you do nothing when people provoke you, most of them feel foolish and stop. You win by ending the assault, even though you did absolutely nothing. The second time, even though you "stand up for yourself," the other person wins and has fun, and a fight is set in motion.

The Game of Life

If you are like most kids, you enjoy playing games. Playing is fun. You know exactly what you are doing and why. And you know when you are winning and when you are losing because the rules are clear.

You may not be used to thinking of life as a game, but it is. Just like in games, there are rules that determine winning and losing. If you know the rules well, you have a better chance of winning. If you win in the game of life you feel good, and if you lose, you feel bad.

Imagine what it would be like if you played a game your whole life and used strategies that made you win. Then the rules were changed so that the same winning strategies now become ways to lose, but no one told you. You'd continue using the same strategies and go completely nuts wondering why you are always losing!

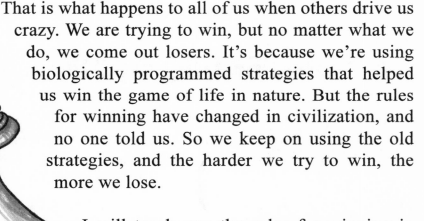

If you want to be a winner, you have to know the rules.

That is what happens to all of us when others drive us crazy. We are trying to win, but no matter what we do, we come out losers. It's because we're using biologically programmed strategies that helped us win the game of life in nature. But the rules for winning have changed in civilization, and no one told us. So we keep on using the old strategies, and the harder we try to win, the more we lose.

I will teach you the rules for winning in civilization. Imagine how great life will be when you know how to win. Life will become simpler and more fun. Since most people are also playing by the wrong rules, you will have a big advantage over them. When you know the rules, it will become almost impossible for you to lose!

What is the most important component to becoming a winner in the game of life? Power. What kind of power? People power. Having people on your side will give you power. Having people against you will weaken you.

Is Power Bad?

You may think power is bad. After all, your bullies have power over you, and that sure doesn't feel good. Maybe you've heard adults say that people who want power are evil. That's because they think power means hurting others or taking unfair advantage of them.

If you believe power is bad you are handicapping yourself. You will have no chance against someone who likes power and knows how to get it.

No one can stop me now.

All living things want power. In nature, creatures that don't try to have power quickly become snacks for more powerful creatures. Since power is necessary for survival, Mother Nature designed us to feel good when we have power and to feel bad when we are powerless.

Perhaps you think of power as beating people up, and you don't want to be a violent person. However, there are many things you do for power *without* hitting anyone. Just think about it. Do you ever argue with your parents, say, over what time to go to bed or when to come home from hanging out with friends? Do you ever fight with a brother or sister over the TV remote control? You may not have realized it, but it's power that you want. Whenever you find yourself in an argument or a fight, you are trying to overpower the other person.

Even when you are doing things everyone considers "good," you are actually seeking power. Do you want good grades in school? Good grades are power. Get higher grades than your classmates, and your teachers and parents will like you, admire you, and want to help you achieve your goals in life. Good grades will get you into a good college so that you can get an important job and make lots of money. Do you want lots of money? Well, money is power. With money you pay other people to help you and make things for you. If you would rather be rich than poor, that means you want power. Don't feel guilty about it. That's just the way life is. Even Mother Theresa asked people for money so she could have the power to accomplish her mission.

Perhaps to your surprise, you will soon see the best way to have power is not by being mean to people but by being nice. So don't worry about power being bad. It's *not* having power that is bad.

Why You Need Power

Okay, so maybe power isn't bad. But why do we need to control others?

Take it back.
You forgot the mushrooms.

The reason is simple. Can you grow, pick and prepare all the food you need for yourself? Can you make your own clothing? Can you make your own house and furniture and toys? Can you teach yourself everything you need to know? Of course not. No one can. The only way we can survive in life is by having others help us.

This is especially true if you are a kid, because you aren't able to perform many of the tasks critical to your survival. You probably don't realize it, but there are slaves working for you round-the-clock without even being told to. These slaves are your parents, and possibly your grandparents or other adult relatives. They feed you, clothe you, give you a roof over your head, provide you with entertainment, drive you around, take care of you when you are sick or hurt, and clean up after you. They do much more for you than you do for them. And there's a good chance that instead of appreciating it, you just get mad at them when they don't give you what you want. You may feel like they try to boss you around. But if you think about it, you will realize you have much more control over them than they have over you.

Even adults need to have power over others because they can't create everything they need to survive by themselves. They go to work and do things for others. Then they get paid so they can pay others to do things for them. In order for society to exist, people have to *give* power to others and *get* power over others. Power over others is necessary for you and for me.

14

The Carrot or the Stick

There are two ways to get power. They are known as "the carrot" and "the stick." Almost all acts of getting power fall into one of these two categories, which refer to how to get a stubborn mule to pull you. You can dangle a carrot in front of the animal and it will move forward, trying to reach the food it wants. Or you can hit its backside with a stick and it will move forward to avoid being hit again.

It's the same thing with people. You can get power over them by making them feel good (offering them the carrot) or by hurting them (hitting them with the stick). If you make them feel good, they want to do things for you to make you happy. If you hurt them, they will fear you and do things for you so that you won't hurt them again.

The carrot approach has advantages over the stick. If you do things that make people feel good, they like you and try to make you happy in return. They may not even realize you are controlling them because they *want* to be doing what they're doing for you. It is also safe because you won't be causing anyone to seek revenge.

If you hurt people, they may give you power over them because they are afraid of you. But they will hate you for hurting them and resent you for controlling them. It also puts you in danger because they will be on the lookout for any opportunity to get even.

In case you haven't realized it yet, the "carrot" is the buddy way to have power and the "stick" is the bully way. Making people feel good turns them into your friends and making them feel bad turns them into your enemies.

You may think you are a good person and that you don't use the bully way to achieve power, but chances are you use it much more often than you think. Do you ever yell or whine or pout when your parents aren't giving you what you want? Do you ever hit your brothers and sisters, or call them names? Do you ever tell your friends you are not going to get together with them if they don't do the activity you want? Do you ever tell the teacher when kids bother you in school? All these are examples of using the stick.

Unfortunately, in real life we can't always use only the carrot. This is especially true when people have to make others obey them. This includes teachers and parents and bosses. Your teachers have to make you work hard many hours a day in school and then at home. They couldn't get you to do all this work just by being nice to you (the carrot). They also have to make you afraid of lousy grades and punishments (the stick).

No one uses only the buddy way or the bully way. We use both. Most of us, though, don't even think about which one we are using. We just go along with our feelings at the moment, or act by habit without considering if it's smart. Far too often, we use the bully way. That's what gets us in trouble. People treat us badly because we don't even realize we are using the stick.

To become a winner, you have to start thinking about when to use the carrot and when to use the stick. First, you will need to recognize the ways you have been using the stick without being aware of it. Then you will have to replace the stick with the carrot. The better you get at giving carrots, the less you will need sticks. You will find people like you better, are nicer to you, and do more for you. (And they won't even guess that you are controlling them!)

The Power Rules in Nature

If using the carrot is so much better than the stick, why do so many of us use the stick? Why do we often get angry and become mean instead of always behaving nicely to each other? Why are there bullies that make us miserable?

Because we are not biologically designed for the environment in which we now live (civilization). We are designed for conditions that prevailed during the earliest period of human history — when the rules for survival were very different from what they are today.

Living in civilization for several thousand years hasn't changed our biological programming. We still experience reactions designed for survival in nature. Let's take a look at the kind of life we are "pre-wired" for.

In nature, we originally lived in tribes of 50 to 100 people. As "cavemen" and "cavewomen," we took refuge in caves and other natural shelters that protected us from the elements. Life was difficult and dangerous. We went from place to place looking for food, without a regular home. We had to be strong to hunt wild animals for our survival, while fighting to prevent them from making us *their* dinner. And we had to defend ourselves from other people and animals competing for the same limited resources.

Hey, give me back my apple! That's stealing!

In the world of nature, "might makes right." In a conflict, the stronger one wins. If I find food and you want it, can I say "Don't take my food! That's stealing!"? In nature there are no laws against stealing. If you are strong enough to take the food away from me, then it's yours to eat. So in those days, "the stick" was very important. The better we could fight, the more others would be afraid of us, and the more likely we were to survive.

As cavemen, we had no democratic elections. The leader of the tribe was the best fighter. If he could beat up the rest of us and keep us afraid, then he was the boss. This would bother us because it meant he got the most of whatever resources were available. However, we probably didn't mind all that much. Since the leader was the No.1 tough guy, when we were attacked by outside enemies, he would be out there on the front lines protecting the rest of us. He would also be leading the hunts, making sure there is enough food for us.

Women had to be tough, too. They had to help defend the tribe against outside enemies when necessary. They had to solve conflicts with their own might, fight for status among the women, and drive away men who were being too aggressive with them.

In our cave days, we had lots of real enemies. People and other animals were constantly looking to harm us, and we had to stop them. We were programmed to get angry and scare them off, or to fight and tear them to pieces before they tore us to pieces. Using "the stick" was essential for survival.

But don't think the stick was the only way to achieve power during those early days. If all the leader did was beat people up and act selfishly, the rest of us would hate him. If there was a tough guy we liked better, we would support his efforts to knock off the leader. So, even in prehistoric times, you had to know how to use the carrot — to make others feel good. If you were a generous and considerate leader, you would lead for a long time.

If you lacked physical strength and couldn't get power by using the stick, you could still have a decent life by getting power with the carrot. If you figured out ways to make lots of people like you, then their power became your power. When you were threatened, attacked, sick or injured, the rest would gladly step in to help you.

Since the carrot and the stick are essential to our survival in nature, Mother Nature programmed us for both. They are part of our instinctual (pre-wired) makeup to this very day. That's why we feel good when other people like us, and we also feel good when others are too afraid of us to try to hurt us.

The Power Rules in Civilization

We are no longer cavemen. Today, we are civilized people. That means we no longer live by the laws of nature. We live by man-made laws of right and wrong.

Civilization developed along with farming. Human beings learned how to grow food and were able to feed more children. It meant we stopped wandering from place to place in search of food and, instead, began living in permanent villages. The better we became at growing food, the more crowded our villages became, creating more opportunities for arguing and fighting.

In the early days of farming, we must have continued to handle our disputes the way we did in nature, by "might makes right." But this resulted in way too much pain and bloodshed, so we created laws, which are rules for handling or preventing conflict without violence. These laws aim to be fair, so we will be willing to live by them. When we have a conflict with someone, instead of slugging it out to see who gets his way, we work it out by the rules. We even created law-enforcement systems, including police, judges and jails, so we can catch and punish you if you don't play according to the rules. In civilization, therefore, "justice makes right."

When we were cavemen, there were about 10 million humans on the planet because there wasn't enough food for more. There was a lot of fighting going on. By killing each other off, the population remained at the level the available food supply could support. Thanks to civilization, there are now over 6 billion people in the world and we rarely have to hit each other. Farming produces enough food for nearly everyone, so we don't have to be enemies. In fact, this is the first period in the history of the world that poor people can be fat! (At least in the more developed countries.) The biggest problem for most people today is not "Where is my next meal going to come from?" but "How do I stop eating so much?"

As cavemen, it was very important to be able to use the stick to hurt and scare others. Civilization made it against the law to use violence to get our way. If we use the stick too hard, instead of getting more power, we get in trouble. We can be arrested and punished and become big losers. Civilization also means we can live without fear that our neighbors are going to hurt us. They know we can call the police on them and then they lose.

Civilization makes it possible for us to become leaders without risking injury. You don't become the leader of a country by beating up everyone else. The carrot has become a lot more important for getting power. You become a leader today by convincing people that you can make them happy — not by making them afraid of you. In our personal lives, too, the more we make people happy, the more powerful we become.

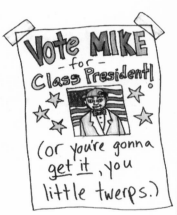

Why Kids Bully Each Other

If civilization makes it possible to have power without harming others, why do people hurt each other? Why is there so much bullying going on?

It's because civilization didn't change our biological nature. The animal instinct to gain power by hurting and scaring others has not disappeared. If you aren't sure about this, just look at what happens when you get angry. Doesn't it seem to happen automatically? Do you think you are offering carrots when you are angry?

Anger is not nice. Getting mad at people doesn't make them feel good or turn them into your friends. It is aggressive behavior. It's the attempt to scare off enemies or to beat them up. In civilization, we continue getting angry even though it almost always makes the situation worse. Our brains are programmed for the dangerous life in nature, when getting angry was necessary for defeating real enemies.

Our brains are still programmed to get power through the stick, by hurting and scaring others. When we were toddlers, practically all of us would bully our parents by screaming, hitting or throwing objects at them to make them do what we want. We would also do these things to our brothers, sisters, cousins and friends. No one taught us these aggressive behaviors. We were just doing what came naturally. In fact, our parents worked hard to teach us *not* to do them.

As we grow up, we discover being mean gets us punished but being nice prevents us from getting in trouble and makes others like us. So we learn to be less aggressive. Some of us, though, prefer to continue using force to be powerful. These people enjoy the power of bossing others around and keeping us scared of them. They are tough and aren't afraid of punishment. Kids like this are often popular because others admire their fearlessness.

When we were living in nature, where toughness and courage were necessary to hunt wild animals and fight enemies, these kids would probably become our leaders. In civilization, though, many of them get in trouble so often that they end up hating teachers and education. Some of them join gangs, take up criminal activities and serve time in jail.

The really smart ones, though, figure out how to be tough and scary without getting in trouble. They will make sure to act respectfully so their teachers will find it hard to believe they could actually bully other kids. If a victim tells on them, the bully's friends will testify that the victim is lying. They get good grades in school and go on to get important jobs. Because they are not afraid of people and know how to make others obey them, they may end up with leadership positions in companies, labor unions or government. Some might become soldiers or policemen or firefighters, open a business or do other things that require toughness and daring. Though we may think bullies are terrible, the truth is that even in civilization bullies are needed for positions that require people who aren't afraid to fight.

There's one big disadvantage caused by civilization. While civilization makes life safer for us, it also makes it easier for people to bully each other and drive each other crazy. In nature, to defeat your opponents, you had to be stronger and meaner than they were. Then they would fear you and leave you alone. But in civilization, someone can be weaker than you and still bully you. How? By using your biological programming against you.

This is how it works: The bullies pick on you, and you get angry, trying to win and make them stop. But they're not really afraid of you because you're not allowed to hit them. You get angrier and angrier in the attempt to win, and don't realize that the angrier you get, the more you lose and look like a fool. So even though you are physically stronger than they are, they can still defeat you by getting you angry and driving you crazy!

1. The best person in the world to make bullies leave you alone is:
    a. The President of the United States
    b. Your mother or father.
    c. The teacher.
    d. The school principal.
    e. You.

2. Victims continue to get picked on by bullies because:
    a. They look different from other people.
    b. They are not as smart as other kids.
    c. They get upset by the bullying.
    d. The school does nothing to stop bullies.

3. When you get angry at bullies, the bullies are most likely to:
    a. Feel bad about what they did and apologize.
    b. Have fun and want to bother you again.
    c. Get scared of you and leave you alone.
    d. Cry.

4. Bullying happens:
    a. To kids in school.
    b. To kids at home.
    c. To adults.
    d. To people of all ages and relationships.

5. The first step to solving problems with other people is:
    a. Blaming them for making you feel bad.
    b. Blaming yourself.
    c. Figuring out what you are doing wrong.
    d. Complaining to adults.

6. When people call you names and you don't try to stop them:
    a. They will feel like losers.
    b. They will feel like winners.
    c. They will try to break your nose.
    d. They will tell the teacher on you.

7. If someone pushes you and you push back, the person will probably:
    a. Feel bad for having pushed you.
    b. Thank you.

    c. Shake your hand.
    d. Push you back even harder.

8. To win the game of life, it is most important to:
    a. Hurt people.
    b. Cheat.
    c. Treat people like friends.
    d. Make people scared of you.

9. Trying to get good grades in school is:
    a. Only for wimps and losers.
    b. A waste of time.
    c. A good way to make people hate you.
    d. A good way to have power.

10. The following word most accurately describes what your parents are for you:
    a. Slaves
    b. Masters
    c. Playmates
    d. Shopkeepers

11. Being able to beat people up is most important for survival in:
    a. Civilization.
    b. School.
    c. Nature.
    d. Camp.

12. In Civilization:
    a. "Justice makes right."
    b. "Might makes wrong."
    c. "Justice makes wrong."
    d. "Might makes right."

13. If we were still living in Nature, kids who were best at fighting and scaring others would probably grow up to be:
    a. Wimps.
    b. Cooks.
    c. Medicine men.
    d. Leaders.

14. To defeat others in Civilization:
    a. You have to be able to beat them up.
    b. You only have to be able to get them mad.
    c. You have to have better clothing than they do.
    d. You have to have bigger muscles than they do.

Section Two: General Rules

The Golden Rule

Stop Thinking of Bullies as "Bad Guys"

Start Thinking of Bullies as "Good Guys"

What Bullies Want

The Worst Way to Get Power

Turning Bullies into Buddies — the Secret

Refuse to Get Mad

Treat Everything as the Words of Your Best Friend

Don't Be Afraid of Bullies

Don't Attack Bullies

Don't Defend Yourself

Don't Tell on Bullies

Show You Are Hurt, Not Angry

Three Points to Remember

Section Two Quiz

The Golden Rule

When someone is nice to us, we feel like being nice back. When someone is mean to us, we feel like being mean back. Nobody taught this to us; it's the way we are designed. Mother Nature programmed us to treat other people the way they treat us. That's because in nature, we had plenty of real enemies that wanted to hurt or kill us. If others were nice to us, it was smart to be their friends in return. It made both of us stronger, especially when there were enemies around that wanted to demolish us. But those who were mean to us were probably looking to hurt or kill us, so it made sense to be even meaner to them than they were to us.

Several thousand years ago, someone had a brilliant idea. If it's our nature to treat others the way they treat us, it must also be *their* nature to treat us the way we treat them. Who needs enemies? Enemies hurt us and make us miserable. So why not force everyone to become our friends? All we have to do is treat others nicely even when they are being mean to us. Before long, they will start treating us back nicely because they are programmed to treat us the way we treat them!

This concept has become known as The Golden Rule: "Treat others as you would like to be treated." This rule is so wonderful that every religion has adopted it in some form, such as, "Love your neighbor as yourself," and "Whatever is hateful to you, do not to others." The Golden Rule is the ultimate rule for having success in civilization. Since civilization provides enough food for everyone, we don't have to be enemies at all. By using The Golden Rule, everyone becomes friends and we all become stronger and happier.

Throughout your life, if you are ever unsure about how to handle a problem with another person, ask yourself if you are using The Golden Rule: *"Am I treating this person the way I would like to be treated?"* or *"Would I like it if they were doing to me what I am doing to them?"* If the answer is "Yes," you will probably solve the problem. If the answer is "No," you will probably get bad results and should change your strategy.

It is not always obvious how to use The Golden Rule. This book should make it clearer for you.

Stop Thinking of Bullies as "Bad Guys"

Do you want to stop being a victim? Then starting right now, get rid of the idea that bullies are "the bad guys" and their victims are "the good guys." Of course, that's not easy to do. Your teachers and parents tell you bullies are bad. But as long as you think bullies are bad, you are going to hate them and treat them like enemies. So they will continue to *be* your enemies — and continue to win.

It may seem obvious that bullies are bad and you are good. But do you think your bullies see it that way? I bet they think they're the good guys and you're the bad one. Who is to say you are right and they are wrong?

Whenever you are angry, you feel like a *victim*. But those you are angry at feel you are a *bully* because your anger is the desire to scare them off or beat them up. So if you go around being angry at your bullies, you probably look like a bad guy.

In fact, many victims are actually accused of being the real bullies. Has this ever happened to you? If so, it probably made you furious because you felt it was unfair. (And your fury makes you look even more like the *real* bad guy). Since you don't like it when others think of you as a bad guy, you have to stop thinking of others as bad guys.

There's an easy way to determine if people who bother you feel they're your bully or your victim. Ask yourself: *Are they angry with me?* If they are, you can be sure they don't like how you are treating them — they feel you are bullying them. This is actually what goes on in most conflicts. Both sides are angry, and each one thinks it's the innocent victim and the other is the guilty bully.

Sometimes adults will decide that *you* are the real bully.

True bullies — those who don't see themselves as victims — are not angry. They are cool and confident while their victims walk around feeling angry.

There are kids who are mean to others and have no friends at all. They may look like bullies, but they are not. They feel like colossal victims. They are so mad at everybody for not liking them, all they want to do is get even. If you know people like that, they need help. (Make sure they read this book!)

It's easy to think of bullies as abnormal, evil creatures designed to hurt us and ruin our lives. The truth is they really are not that different from the rest of us. They want exactly what we want: to be winners in life. We all want power. We all want respect. And we all want to be popular. The difference between bullies and their victims is that the bullies are better at getting what they want. Thinking of people as good guys and bad guys may help us feel better, but it is much more helpful to think of people as winners and losers.

Just about everyone we call bullies are buddies to their friends. Bullies protect their buddies and enjoy being tough enough to stand up against others. If they thought of you as a friend, they would fight for you, too!

We may not want to admit it, but bullies tend to have a trait we admire: courage. What they do may not be smart, but they have the guts to challenge other people. Of course, it doesn't take much courage to pick on smaller and weaker kids, but many bullies stand up to bigger and stronger kids, too. They are even willing to risk punishment from adults who take the side of the victims.

Start Thinking of Bullies as "Good Guys"

To turn your bullies into buddies, you have to start thinking of them as "good guys." Strange as it may sound, I want you to tell yourself they are doing you a favor when they bully you.

You may be thinking, *"Are you nuts? They're doing me a favor when they bully me? They're destroying my life!"*

I know it sounds crazy. But think for a minute about professional boxers. Boxers want to become great fighters and develop the skills to win. Do you think they will ever succeed without someone to spar against? Of course not. They need sparring partners who are willing to go into the ring and slug it out with them.

Do boxers *hate* their sparring partners? Do you think they are mad at them for hitting back and trying to knock them out? Do they wish a truck would run them over so they'll never be able to hurt them again? No. They need sparring partners. Without this kind of practice, they will never become successful boxers.

The same thing is true with your bullies. Think of them as your sparring partners in the game of life, and they will help you train to be a winner. Remember, people are going to try to bully you throughout your life. The sooner you learn how to deal with them, the sooner your life as a winner will begin.

Therefore, I want you to see your bullies as your sparring partners. Be grateful to them for giving you the chance to practice your skills. If it weren't for them, you would not be reading this book and learning how to become a winner with people for the rest of your life.

Taking on bullies may not always go smoothly. You're likely to make mistakes in the beginning, but that's how life is. The professional boxer doesn't win every time. If you lose, don't get mad at the bullies. Just do your best to win the next time.

There's another reason to think of bullies as good guys. Until now they have been mean to you, so you think of them as bad. Would you feel the same way if instead of hurting you they protected you? Of course not. Your goal is to turn your bullies into buddies. When you succeed, they will indeed be good in your eyes. To start that process, all you have to do is begin thinking of them as good. The sooner you do, the quicker you'll start to win.

What Bullies Want

Remember, the best way to have power today is by offering carrots. If you understand what bullies want and make them happy, they will stop making you miserable. They can even become your friends.

Remember the three things bullies want: power, respect and popularity. These are exactly the same things everyone wants, including you. The difference lies in how they go about getting these things.

There are two ways bullies can have power. One way is by having people on their side. The other way is to have people against them but *scared* of them. This gives the bullies the power and they are the winners.

When bullies are mean to you, they are really testing you. They want to know if you are *for* them or *against* them. They could do this by being nice to you, and you would be on their side. But if they do this, they are making the test too easy. Why *wouldn't* you be on their side if they're nice to you? So the real test is if you are on their side even if they are mean to you. If you get mad at them, you fail the test. You prove you are against them and that you deserve to be treated badly. If you tell on them and try to get them in trouble, then you have wiped out any doubt that you are an enemy.

On the other hand, if you don't respond with anger, you have passed the bully's test. They see that you don't hurry to consider them enemies just because they're trying to demonstrate power over you. The same thing is true when parents and teachers are mean to you. Because of their roles, they need to make you obey them. If you get mad when they try to control you, they will see you as defiant and be tougher on you. But if you accept their authority, they will know you are on their side and treat you better.

Parents will give you much more freedom when you show them respect.

Bullies want respect. Everyone does. If you get mad at them, you are *dis*respecting them. They won't like you and will try to make you suffer. However, if you give them respect they will like you. It is not necessary to do everything bullies tell you to do, even when the bullies are parents and teachers. However, you do need to show them respect. Show them respect and you will be amazed by what they let you get away with. They will actually be happier if you disobey them respectfully than if you obey them rudely!

The third thing bullies want is popularity. We all do. True bullies — those who don't see themselves as victims — are usually quite popular. They know how to use both the carrot and the stick. They make people like them by protecting them and making them feel "in" with the cool guy. But bullies also act mean to other kids so their followers will admire their toughness and lack of fear of punishment. And their buddies will know they'd better be loyal or they'll become victims, too.

Bullies love to see you as the enemy and make you terrified of them. It increases their popularity. But if you play the enemy role, it makes you a big loser. There's another way to satisfy bullies' desire for popularity: Put yourself on their side. You also count as a person and your "vote" matters. Remember, supporting bullies doesn't mean that you make them your boss and do whatever they tell you. All you have to do is show them respect and they will like you and respect you in return. Later on in this book, you will learn just how to do that. I will also teach you how to be on the bully's side without being against anyone else.

The Worst Way to Get Power

Making friends is not the only way to have power. Another way is to make people suffer. In a conflict, the winner is the one who comes out feeling the best and the loser is the one who feels the worst. So if you make somebody feel worse than you, you are the one with the greater power.

There are different ways to make people suffer. Some of the most common ones are:

1. Hurting their feelings

2. Hurting their bodies

3. Hurting their reputations

4. Damaging or stealing their possessions

5. Getting them in trouble

6. Making them afraid of you

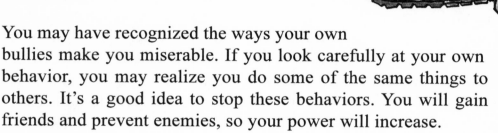

I sure showed her who's boss!

All of these methods give you power. At the same time, they turn people into your enemies, so you also *lose* power. You never know when people you have hurt will turn around and get back at you and turn you into a big loser. Even if you are bigger and stronger than they are, they can find ways to get revenge.

You may have recognized the ways your own bullies make you miserable. If you look carefully at your own behavior, you may realize you do some of the same things to others. It's a good idea to stop these behaviors. You will gain friends and prevent enemies, so your power will increase.

The only possible exception is item No. 6 — making people afraid of you. It can be helpful to have some people afraid of you. They won't want to hurt you or make you mad. They will do what you tell them because they are afraid of you. But this will work only if you are a really scary person. Chances are if you were such a person, you wouldn't be reading this book.

It is only safe to have people afraid of you if you also treat them like friends. If you are scaring people while treating them like enemies, they will try to get revenge when the opportunity presents itself. But if they see you as a friend, they will think they are listening to you because they *want* to make you happy, not because they are terrified of what you can do to them.

In some situations, it is even *necessary* to use fear to control people. For instance, if you are a teacher, parent, boss or police officer, your role requires you to make people obey you. If students weren't afraid of getting lousy report cards or being sent to detention, do you think they'd work so hard in school all day long and then go home to study and do homework?

Turning Bullies into Buddies — the Secret

This is how you will:

1. Prevent yourself from having enemies

2. Stop people from fighting with you

3. Turn yourself into a winner

4. Get more respect

These rules will work with anyone. They work with other kids. They'll work with brothers and sisters. You can even use them on your parents. Each rule will be explained in a chapter of its own.

Rule 1: Refuse to get mad.

Rule 2: Treat everything as the words of your best friend.

Rule 3: Don't be afraid of bullies.

Rule 4: Don't attack bullies.

Rule 5: Don't defend yourself.

Rule 6: Don't tell on bullies.

Rule 7: Show you are hurt, not angry.

Refuse to Get Mad

Question: Is anger a feeling we have toward friends or enemies?

Answer: Anger is not a nice, pleasant, friendly feeling. It is what we feel toward an enemy. We feel we are being attacked and we want to scare or hurt our opponent.

Even when we're mad at good friends, at that moment we feel they are acting like our enemies. This makes them mad right back at us, so they treat us like an enemy, too.

Question: When someone bothers us and we get mad, who is the loser?

Answer: We are. To defeat us, people don't have to break our bones or make us bleed. All they have to do is make us mad. When we are mad, we feel miserable and they feel good. Since everyone wants to win, they will keep on doing exactly what gets us mad.

Because we don't want to turn people into enemies, and we don't want to be losers, we have to refuse to give them the power to make us angry.

You may be thinking, *"But how can I just decide to stop being mad and upset when people are mean to me?"*

When people treat us badly, we get angry. This is an automatic response programmed into our brains. It feels like our bullies have a remote control to our brain and they're pressing the "anger button" to make us mad.

But bullies do not really push buttons to control our brains. It just feels like that because of the way Mother Nature programmed us. She gave us the automatic response of getting angry to help us against enemies when we were living in the dangerous world of nature. When you get mad, do you *decide* to get mad? Do you tell yourself, *"I think getting angry is the smart thing to do in this situation because it will help me win"*? Of course not. Since you get angry without thinking about it, it *feels* like others make you angry.

Today we live in civilization, where life is much safer. We don't have to hunt or fight to survive. In fact, there are very strict laws against fighting, so there is a good chance that fighting will get us in deep trouble.

You may *want* to punch your bullies in the nose, but you are not allowed to. Your opponents can do all kinds of things to get you mad without being afraid that you will hurt them. They can laugh while you get angrier and angrier. The angrier you get, the more you become the loser.

So tell yourself the only way to win is by *not* getting mad! Disable the "anger button" in your brain. Show your bullies they can try all they want, but they can't get you mad! This is really not so hard to do once you realize it. There are many things our bodies do without our awareness but we can still control them if we wish. When you see something funny, your automatic response is to laugh, but you can easily stop yourself from laughing. If a doctor tests your reflexes by tapping below your knee with a hammer, your leg will automatically respond by kicking, but you can decide not to let your leg kick. And when people are mean to you, the natural response is to get angry, but you can decide not to.

Arrrr Loser. Arrrrr. Paul is a Loser.

It will be easier to control your anger if you get rid of the idea that bullies "have no right" to be mean to you. Of course, they don't have the right to commit *crimes* against you, like injuring you or stealing from you, but there is no law forcing them to be *nice*. If you believe that people have no right to be mean to you, you will become angry whenever they aren't nice. But if you realize people *do* have a right to be mean, you won't automatically get mad when they are nasty.

1. Thou Shalt wait thy turn
2. Thou shalt laugh politely at people's jokes
3. Thou shalt say "please" and "thank you"

When you refuse to get mad, your bullies will discover they can no longer defeat you. They will feel like fools and losers every time they pick on you. Before long, they won't even *try* to get you upset because they don't want to lose. You will become the winner without doing anything against them. And you will get respect, because you are the winner, not the loser.

Another strange thing will happen. The bullies will start liking you better when they see they can't defeat you. Why? For three basic reasons:

1. *You are no longer mad at them.* People don't like you when you are mad at them. When you stop being angry, they won't have a reason to be angry either.

2. *They can respect you now.* You want friends you can respect. Your bullies are no different. If you get mad, they can't respect you because you are the loser. When they can no longer defeat you, they will respect you more. Then it will be much easier for them to become your friends.

3. *You are showing them respect.* Your bullies enjoy respect just as much as you do. When you no longer get angry, you are treating the bullies with more respect. And they will like you better for it!

Treat Everything as the Words of Your Best Friend

This is an absolutely wonderful and powerful rule for having good relationships. It sounds kind of crazy, but it works beautifully and you should use it with everyone in your life. Tell yourself that everything people tell you, no matter how nasty or angry they sound, is the words of your best friend. Tell yourself that the only reason they are talking to you like this is because they love you, care about you, and want to help you.

Oh boy, so much good free advice!

This doesn't mean you have to treat them as if they are right, or that you have to do whatever they tell you. All it means is that you consider them to have nothing but good intentions. Be grateful for everything they have to say to you.

If someone calls you stupid, tell yourself they are saying it not because they want to hurt your feelings but because they want to help you be smarter. So how could you be mad at them? Or if they call you a fatso, it is because they are trying to encourage you to go on a diet. So be appreciative.

If your parents call you a spoiled brat, don't get mad at them. Realize they are trying to get you to act more maturely, and then it will be easier for them to give you more of what you want.

On the other hand, if people urge you to shoplift, don't do it just because you're considering them to be your best friends. Tell yourself they are trying to help you have things you can't afford, but you can't do it because it is illegal and against your beliefs.

Or if someone tells you to jump off a tall building, you shouldn't do it just because you are considering them friends who love you. But you should tell yourself they must have a very good reason for saying it. Maybe it's their way of hinting that you are acting like a jerk and would do everyone a favor by stopping.

Don't forget that your goal is to be a winner by having as many friends and as few enemies as possible. And if you *think* of people as your friends, they are more likely to *be* your friends.

Don't Be Afraid of Bullies

"What do you mean, don't be afraid of bullies? The bullies are scary! They ridicule me in front of everyone! They hurt my feelings. They threaten me and hit me!"

Question: Are we afraid of friends, or are we afraid of enemies?

Answer: Fear, of course, is something we feel toward enemies. Friends don't want to hurt us, so there's no need to fear them. Therefore, by being afraid of bullies, we are treating them like enemies. So they'll treat us like enemies. Our bullies will never stop bullying us as long as we continue to be afraid of them.

Question: If we are afraid of someone, who is in the stronger position?

Answer: The other person is. So by being afraid of someone, we put ourselves in the weaker position. We automatically lose and don't get respect. Since everyone wants to be a winner, our bullies will continue doing whatever makes us afraid.

"But how can I just stop being afraid? The bullies are dangerous and can hurt me."

If we were still living in caveman days, then you would be smart to be afraid of bullies. There was real, serious fighting going on then, and no one went to jail for beating someone up.

But now we live in civilization. We have tons of rules against hurting people, and there are policemen and courts and prisons to make sure the rules are followed. When we are in school, the school staff does a pretty good job of enforcing the same rules. (Chances are you do a lot less fighting in school than you do at home with your brothers and sisters!) The law is like an invisible shield to protect us. If bullies injure us, it is easy to get them in serious trouble and they lose big time.

Don't assume that bullies are stupid. They don't want to get in trouble. But fortunately for them, there is an easy way for them to defeat you without physically hurting you. They play a game with you called "Let's Scare People." If you get scared, you lose.

It's easy for them to scare us by taking advantage of the fact that our brains still work like cavemen brains. We are programmed to respond to their threats as though they really *are* going to hurt us. In caveman times, being afraid was important for survival. Our fear kept us out of fights with people who could hurt us. While we're no longer in real danger from bullies, our brains still respond as though we are. So bullies keep on scaring us, even though they probably don't intend to injure us, and they win.

But you want to be a winner, so you must decide to stop being afraid of bullies. Even if they are bigger and stronger than you, don't worry. You aren't in real danger. Most of them are not the evil villains you have been imagining them to be. They are just playing around with you. When you stop being afraid of them, they feel foolish trying to scare you and soon stop. Then they cease being your enemies and are free to be your friends.

So when you find your body telling you, *"Oh, no, the bullies are so big and strong! I'm afraid they are going to hurt me,"*

Bullies are rarely as dangerous as they seem.

Walgreen's Photo

walgreens.com

username is same as email
um   rpreefer@yahoo.com

password is
roylea

8.4.78

catch yourself and realize that this fear makes you automatically lose. Instead, tell yourself something like this:

"They are bigger and stronger than I am, but they can't hurt me. I'm not strong enough to beat them up by myself, but that's okay because I don't have to. There is an invisible shield protecting me, and if they go through this shield, the law is going to punish them and I am going to win. So they can act as scary as they want, and it doesn't bother me in the least!"

It's not enough just to stop being scared of people who threaten you. It is also essential not to get mad at them, either, or you'll end up enemies. So be perfectly calm. Don't give them any dirty looks. Smile instead. Tell yourself that people have every right in the world to try to scare you, and you are not going to take this right away from them. Since they're not doing anything wrong, you have no reason to be mad at them. With this attitude, you will discover that people like you and respect you, and that you have no enemies, no matter how small or weak you may be. In fact, if you have no fear and anger, they may even admire you and want to act as your protectors, *especially* if you are small and weak! So stop being afraid of them, and you just might get yourself some free bodyguards!

Warning: *There is, of course, a chance that someone is so angry with you that he will actually try to harm you physically. How can you judge if you are in real danger or not? Very simply: by asking yourself if the person threatening you has ever injured you or anyone else before. Someone who has injured people in the past may do so again. People who go around injuring others and aren't afraid of getting in trouble are dangerous. They are more than bullies. They are criminals. With such people, your natural fear is healthy. Be afraid of them, and stay far away from them. If you must be near them, make sure you have people around who can protect you. However, if the person you are afraid of has never hurt anyone (to the best of your knowledge), then you probably don't have to worry that he will hurt you, so don't be scare*d.

Making us afraid that they will hurt our bodies is not the only way people can have power over us. Another simple way is by getting us to fear what they *think* of us. We are terrified that we will look bad in the eyes of others. We want their approval, and we don't feel happy until we get it. The origin of this fear is also in nature. When we were living in tribes in the jungle, there was no Welfare Department and no homeless shelters. We all had to cooperate to survive. What the group thought of us was very important. If the tribe didn't approve of us, they would ridicule us, beat us up or abandon us, and we wouldn't survive for long.

How do you like my hat, Frankie? How about the way I'm standing?

However, in civilization there is no such danger. No matter what our friends think of us, we are going to have food to eat, a bed to sleep in, schools to learn in, and hospitals to take care of us when we are sick. Therefore our basic survival doesn't depend on what others think of us. Our bodies, though, don't know this and react as though we're still in the lawless jungle. In civilization, when we care what others think of us, we are giving them power over us for nothing. Think of it this way: If I care about what you think of *me*, but you don't care what I think of *you*, who is in a stronger position? You are, of course! I will be trying to act or dress in a way I hope you will approve of, while you are doing absolutely nothing for me. You are the one in control. It's like I'm making you my boss. I become the big loser, and losers don't get respect.

Think about the really famous, successful, or powerful people in the world. Do they care what you personally think about them? No. They live their lives the way they want. They will only do what it takes to get you to buy their products or services or, if they're politicians, to vote for them. Many celebrities will purposely behave or dress outrageously. They know we will be so impressed by their daring and originality that we will want to be like them and spend money on their performances or products.

If you want to be happy and successful, stop being concerned that others will think badly of you. All that should matter is that you are acting in a way that you think is right. To win the approval game that people play with you, tell yourself something like this:

"People can think anything they want about me, and it's perfectly OK. I don't mind if they think I'm ugly, stupid, fat, nerdy or gay. This is my life, and I'm going to live it according to my own beliefs and desires."

You will discover that the less you worry what others think of you, the happier and more powerful you become. People will actually respect you more and like you better when they can't control you, and you live by your own values rather than by theirs. As long as you are not hurting them, of course.

There's another thing you should understand about the kids who tease you.

Since they are making fun of you, it seems like they hate you for being different, and if you were just like them, they would love you.

But it only *seems* that way. The truth is they are happy you are different. Part of us wants to be the same as everyone else so that we won't stick out and be made fun of. But deep down, another part of us wants to be different from everyone so that we can feel special. If you were just like your bullies, that wouldn't please them! You would be preventing them from feeling special. And you wouldn't like it, either, because *you* wouldn't be special.

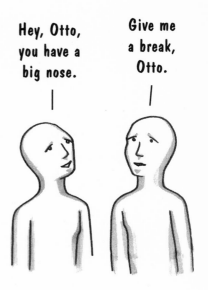

Hey, Otto, you have a big nose.

Give me a break, Otto.

If everyone was the same

If people were all the same, life would be horribly boring. Even more importantly, the world couldn't function if everyone were the same. You need people with different abilities and characteristics to do all the different jobs that are required to keep society running. So feel different, and feel special. Love others for being different from you, and they will love you for being different from them.

By the way, did you ever hear the expression, "Opposites attract"? Well, there's a lot of truth to that. In fact, the kids who tease you may be drawn to you because they are attracted by your being so different from them. You just can't see it because they are trying to make themselves feel good by making you feel bad. So don't fall into the trap of getting upset when they make fun of your differences, and they won't continue to bother you. Maybe they'll end up being your friends because they find your differences so interesting!

Don't Attack Bullies

Question: Do we attack friends or enemies?

Answer: Attacking is something we do to enemies. If we attack bullies, even if they attacked us first, we are letting them know we consider them enemies. So we can expect them to treat us like enemies.

In nature, if an enemy attacks us and we can't escape, it becomes necessary to attack back. The alternative may be death. The instinct to attack was built into our genes from the time we were cavemen. It was necessary in order to have a chance of surviving against enemies who really wanted to harm us or kill us.

But we now live in civilization. It is against the law to hurt others. The bullies know this, and they are not trying to send us to the hospital. We don't have to counterattack in order to win because we are not in real danger from the bullies. If we attack them in return, they will want to attack back even harder. Of course, it is possible that the bullies will become scared of us and leave us alone from then on. But there is a much greater chance that the fight will just get worse, and we may get seriously hurt.

You should assume that your bullies are not stupid. They don't want to get in trouble. They want *you* to get in trouble, so they do a clever trick by using your biological instincts against you. They push you or hit you quietly when the teacher isn't looking. They hope you will instinctively get mad and attack them back so loudly that everyone notices you. You end up getting punished even though the bully started! Or they may hit you back even harder, claiming that you started. By attacking back, instead of becoming a winner, you become a king-sized loser.

I hope you have already tried the Physical Bullying Experiment with at least a few people and found out how nicely it works. It is very hard for a bully to keep on attacking you if you are doing nothing back. Even though it seems like you are "letting the bullies get away with it," you are really defeating them. Bullies feel stupid for attacking someone who isn't fighting back. It also makes you look tough because you can take a push or a hit and it doesn't faze you.

There is another important principle that I want you to learn from this. Everyone thinks that in a fight, the first person to hit is the one who started the fight. The truth is that the *second* person to hit really started the fight! Does this sound nutty! But it's not. It takes two people to make a fight. When someone hits you, there is no fight yet. As you discovered in the experiment, if you do nothing back, no fight happens. It's only when you attack back that a fight erupts! So yes, even though you are the second person to hit, you actually are the one who started the fight.

Warning: *This rule does not apply if you are facing someone who is intent on injuring you no matter what you do, and you are backed in a corner with no one to rescue you. If attacking back is your only chance for preventing serious harm to yourself, of* *course you must do it. Please remember, though, that this is an extremely rare situation that may never happen to you. If people are truly looking to injure you, they're either criminals or you must have given them a mighty good reason for hating you — like telling on them and getting them in trouble!*

Don't Defend Yourself

Does this sound strange? It may make sense to you that attacking bullies is wrong, but why shouldn't you *defend* yourself from them? Are you to simply let them to walk all over you like a doormat?

Question: Do we defend ourselves from friends or from enemies?

Answer: Obviously, we defend ourselves from enemies. We don't need to defend ourselves from friends because friends don't want to hurt us.

Therefore, if we defend ourselves from bullies, it means that we consider them enemies. So they will never be our friends.

Question: If one person is attacking and the other is defending himself, who is in the stronger position?

Answer: The attacker is in the stronger position. It is not fun to have to defend yourself. The attacker has everything to gain and the defender has everything to lose. The best the defender can hope to accomplish is to maintain his or her position. When we defend ourselves we are trying to win the conflict. However, it's impossible to win by defense. It puts the attacker on top and defender at the bottom. The harder we defend ourselves, the bigger we lose, and the bully will continue attacking to force us into the losing defensive position.

If you don't want to be the loser and you don't want to have enemies, you must decide not to defend yourself when someone attacks you. You will get more respect because you will not be the loser. The bullies will like you better because you'll be treating them like friends instead of enemies.

But won't you get hurt if you don't defend yourself?

First take into account that most of the attacks against us are verbal attacks, with words, not with sticks and stones. We certainly don't have to worry about defending ourselves from words.

I'm not being aggressive. I'm only defending myself.

When the attack is physical, of course there is a chance of getting hurt. However, you have a much greater chance of getting hurt when you defend yourself. Why? Because attacking and defending are both acts of fighting. By defending yourself, you are agreeing to participate in fighting. Defense is the weaker position. When you defend yourself, you increase the bullies' confidence. They feel they have the upper hand, so they attack you even harder. The fight escalates and you may end up hurt.

It takes two people to make a fight. When you don't defend yourself, there can't be a fight. The bullies quickly feel stupid attacking people who aren't defending themselves, and then stop trying.

Warning: *As with the previous chapter's rule against attacking bullies, the rule against defending yourself does not apply when the attacker is absolutely determined to harm you. In such a case, not defending yourself will make it easier for them to hurt you. So you must defend yourself to avoid being physically injure*d. *Just remember that in almost all situations, bullies are not looking to send you to the hospital. They are trying to have power over you by making you angry, scared or miserable. Most of the things they do will not hurt you.*

Don't Tell on Bullies

Have adults been urging you to tell them when other kids tease or bully you? Have they been telling you that "Telling is not tattling"?

Please do not take such advice. Telling on bullies, except under rare circumstances, is about the worst thing you can do. The best way to make people despise you without actually committing a crime against them is by trying to get them in trouble with the authorities. This is true whether you are telling your teacher on other students, your parents on your brother or sister, your boss on a coworker, or the police on your neighbor. The harder your bullies get punished, the more intensely they are going to hate you. And they will be burning to get back at you, either by hurting you again or by getting *you* in trouble.

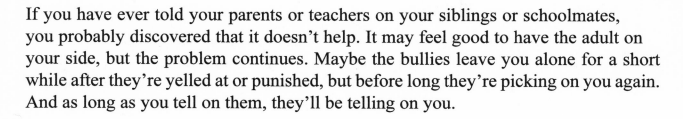

If it is a mistake to tell on bullies, why are the adults saying you must do it? It's because they care for kids and really want to help them. They want to be your heroes fighting off the evil bullies. They just don't realize that their efforts to help may not work. In fact, when adults try to help kids in their conflicts with each other, the fighting almost always gets worse. Since both kids want the adult on their side, they each argue even harder to convince the adult they are right and their opponent is wrong.

If you have ever told your parents or teachers on your siblings or schoolmates, you probably discovered that it doesn't help. It may feel good to have the adult on your side, but the problem continues. Maybe the bullies leave you alone for a short while after they're yelled at or punished, but before long they're picking on you again. And as long as you tell on them, they'll be telling on you.

When the adults confront your bullies, do the bullies simply say, "Oh, yes, I'm guilty. I'm sorry. I won't do it again"? Sometimes they do. But more often they start blaming you and trying to get you in trouble. If the adults are attempting to be fair, there is a good chance they will decide that you are the guilty one. And if the bullies are popular, more kids will testify for them than for you. This makes you look like the real bully. You end up in trouble and being the big loser.

Do you like it when your brother or sister tells your parents on you? Of course not! Your parents are the most important people in the world to you. You want them to love you and be on your side. When your siblings get you in trouble with your parents, you get real mad at your siblings *and* your parents.

When you are in school, it is the same thing. The teacher is the most important person in your school day. The last thing you want is for other kids to get the teacher against you.

Well, your bullies are no different from you. When you tell on them, they'd like to see you get struck by lightning. So remember The Golden Rule. If you don't want them to tell on you, you shouldn't tell on them, either.

Anthony, that was so brave of you to tell on Sam.

Do you want respect? Do you want to be a winner? Of course you do. Well, no one gets the admiration of classmates by telling the teacher on other kids. When you tell on kids who bother you, you are letting everyone know that you can't handle your bullies by yourself. You are declaring that you are weaker than they are, that they are defeating you, and that you need a grown-up's help to win. Even if you get the bullies punished, you still lose because everyone knows you can't do it by yourself. Even the teachers who help you don't truly respect you. They would admire you much more if you solved your bully problem on your own. In fact, people will respect you more if you deal with bullies by yourself and *lose* than if you get an adult to defeat them for you. So when you tell on bullies, you look like a loser, and losers don't get respect.

There are only two instances when you should tell on people: If they have committed a crime, or to prevent a crime. By a crime I mean something that actually causes harm to someone's body or possessions. No one has a right to make you bleed or break your bones. For this they should be punished so they won't want to do it again. They are not allowed to break or steal your possessions. If they do, and are not willing to pay you back or return the items, then you should tell the authorities. If you have good reason to believe that someone is going to harm someone else, then it may be necessary to tell the authorities so they can prevent the crime from happening.

But don't try to get kids in trouble for hurting your feelings. It is not a crime. Whether your feelings are hurt depends upon you, not the other people, so it is wrong to punish them. Don't tell on them if they call you names, spread rumors, or hit you without harming you. (In later chapters you will learn how to handle these situations effectively).

But there is someone you *should* tell if a bully does something you don't like. Who? The bully himself. Think of it this way. Let's say you did something to me that hurt. When will you like me better? If I tell the authorities, or if I tell *you*? Of course you would prefer that I tell you instead of trying to get you in trouble. You will respect me more for having the guts or the decency to talk to you, and you will like me more for not trying to get you in trouble. You are much more likely to apologize and stop bothering me if I tell you than if I tell your teacher, parent, or a policeman. Well, the bullies are just like you. If you need to tell, tell the bully, not the authorities. Just be sure that when you talk to the bully, you are not angry or threatening. Talk the way you would to a good friend. I can't guarantee that your bullies will always listen to you, but I can assure you that the results will be better if you tell them than if you tell *on* them.

Show You Are Hurt, Not Angry

It happens all the time. People hurt us and we get angry. But instead of apologizing and never hurting us again, they get mad and keep hurting us. Why?

If people hurt you, how do you want them to feel about it? You want them to feel *sorry*. You want them to apologize and say they won't do it again. Then you can forgive them and go on being friends.

If you get mad at the people who hurt you, you show them *anger*. So they will probably respond with anger. Do you want people to be *angry* with you when they hurt you? Of course not. You want them to be *sorry*. But when you get mad, instead of making them feel sorry, you make them feel like they're under attack, so they get angry right back.

Why do we make this mistake? Because it is programmed into us by Mother Nature herself. As cavemen, if you hurt me there was a very good chance you would hurt me even more. Maybe you were trying to beat me up and take over my position in the tribe. Or maybe you were a wild animal trying to make me your breakfast. I had to get angry to scare you off or to tear you to pieces before you tore me to pieces. Because it helped us survive, Mother Nature made sure that we would get angry when another creature caused us pain.

But we now live in civilization. You are not an enemy looking to eat me. The law forbids you from injuring me; and if you do injure me, it is probably an accident. Getting angry at you will not do me any good. Just the opposite: It will make you angry back and we may end up enemies.

From now on, if people hurt you, do not make the mistake of getting angry. Just let them know that you are hurt. They will probably feel bad for hurting you. Then they will apologize and avoid hurting you again, which is exactly what you want.

This rule works well with friends, relatives and people who care about you. Kids who have been angry at you for a long time may be happy to see that you are hurt and will want to hurt you again. What should you do about them?

Until now, you have been in a state of war with your bullies. If you have been mad at them, they are mad at you; and if you have been telling on them, they hate you. They may want to make you suffer *now*, but they won't feel this way forever. When you turn your bullies into buddies, they will stop taking pleasure in your pain.

To get the right effect, it has to be clear that you are in serious pain and not just feeling sorry for yourself. If you are able to talk at the time, look the bully in the eyes, imagine him or her to be your best friend, and say something like, "That really hurt." But don't sound angry or the bullies will not feel sorry for hurting you. Don't cry like a baby or sadly walk away like a puppy with its tail between its legs, either. This will make you look like a wimp and a loser, and they will not care about you.

Remember, most bullies are really not heartless. They are basically no different from you and me. They do not enjoy injuring people who aren't trying to hurt them. They simply want to have power. They don't have a remote control to your brain that forces you to feel bad. When they say things and your feelings get hurt, you are really hurting yourself. Stop doing it. It's not fair to blame them when you hurt yourself; they are right to have little sympathy for you. However, if they make you bleed or break your bones, they probably feel terrible. So let your bully know you are hurt when the pain is physical.

Three Points to Remember

To succeed in turning your bullies into buddies you need to avoid falling into traps that will make the bullying continue.

1. The bullying will get worse before it gets better.

Wouldn't it be wonderful if all you had to do is read this book and then you would never be picked on again? Well, it's almost that simple, but not quite. In fact, you must be prepared for the bullying to get *worse* before it gets better. But only for a couple of days.

When you change your attitude, your tormentors will discover you aren't getting upset. They'll feel confused. They'll think something is terribly wrong with you. Maybe you went blind and don't see them. Maybe you went deaf and don't hear them. They won't like the sensation that they aren't winning. But they really *want* to upset you, so they will probably try even harder. They figure if they annoy you long enough, eventually they'll get to you.

After a while, they will become tired of feeling stupid and will stop bothering you. A little later they will try again, hoping you are back to your old self and will get upset. Again, it won't work.

So when you see the harassment intensifying, don't think, *"Oh, no, this isn't working! The bullying is only getting worse!"* It *is* working. It's just that your bullies have been upsetting you for a long time, and they don't want the fun to end. Plus, you have been letting them know all along that the bullying bothers you, and they need some time to figure out that it doesn't anymore.

2. You must follow these instructions 100% of the time.

The only way to succeed in stopping your tormentors is to follow the instructions in this book — all the time. If bullies see you get upset even only once in while, they will know bullying really does bother you; they just have to try harder and more often. So the abuse won't stop. It may even get worse. Only when bullies learn they can *never* get you upset will they stop trying to bother you altogether.

3. Bullies won't disappear.

Follow the instructions in this book and your situation will improve dramatically. But don't expect you'll never get picked on again in your life. Everyone gets picked on once in a while, and there's nothing in the world we can do to change that. The difference is that it will happen much less often than it used to, and the same individual won't bother you more than once or twice. Most importantly, it won't upset you. In fact, it may even make you laugh.

1. The Golden Rule means that:
   a. You should own more gold than other people.
   b. You should only be nice to people when they are nice to you.
   c. You should be nice to people even when they are mean to you.
   d. People should be punished when they are mean to you.

2. To stop being a victim, it is important to start thinking of bullies as:
   a. Good guys.
   b. Bad guys.
   c. Idiots.
   d. Just jealous.

3. When you get angry:
   a. You feel like a bully but look like a victim.
   b. You feel stupid but look smart.
   c. You feel like a victim but look like a bully.
   d. Feel smart and look smart.

4. The way to grow up tough and strong is to:
   a. Never experience any hardship.
   b. Have adults protect you from mean kids.
   c. Watch lots of television.
   d. Have experience dealing with hardship.

5. Parents and teachers will like you better when you:
   a. Disobey them respectfully.
   b. Obey them rudely.
   c. Tell them they are unfair.
   d. Disobey them rudely.

6. If you want kids to stop being your enemies, you should:
   a. Warn them you'll get them in trouble if they are mean to you.
   b. Treat them the way they treat you.
   c. Give them whatever they want.
   d. Show them respect.

7. Anger is the emotion you feel toward:
   a. An enemy.
   b. A friend.
   c. Food.
   d. Clothing.

8. To prevent anger, you should adopt the attitude that:
   a. "No one has a right to be mean to me."
   a. "Life has to be fair."
   c. "I must never be a loser."
   d. "People do have a right to be mean to me."

9. Getting angry will make people:
   a. Like you.
   b. Respect you.
   c. Be angry back at you.
   d. Want to give you what you want.

10. When people call you stupid, you should:
    a. Call them stupid back.
    b. Tell the teacher.
    c. Tell them you aren't stupid.
    d. Be grateful to them for encouraging you to be smarter.

11. If you are afraid of people, you are treating them like:
    a. Enemies.
    b. Friends.
    c. Cousins.
    d. Teachers.

12. You shouldn't fear bullies because:
    a. They only want to scare you.
    b. They probably aren't looking to hurt you.
    c. They don't want to get in trouble.
    d. All of the above.

13. To get the most respect from people, you must:
    a. Live by your own values.
    b. Try hard to get their approval.
    c. Be afraid of what they'll think of you.
    d. Tell on them when they do something you don't like.

14. If everyone were the same:
    a. People would be happier.
    b. Life would be more fun.
    c. We couldn't feel special.
    d. We would all be nicer to each other.

15. A kid pushes you when the teacher isn't looking. You get mad and push back, saying, "Get your hands off of me!" Who is most likely to get in trouble?
    a. The kid who pushed you.
    b. Both of you.
    c. The teacher.
    d. You.

16. If someone is looking to hurt you no matter what you do, you should:
    a. Let them hurt you.
    b. Defend yourself or get help.
    c. Cry.
    d. Spit on them.

17. If people criticize you and you defend yourself, you are:
    a. Treating them like friends.
    b. Being nice to them.
    c. Sounding smart.
    d. Treating them like enemies.

18. When there is an attacker and a defender, the defender is in:
    a. The weaker position.
    b. The stronger position.
    c. The more enjoyable position.
    d. The smarter position.

19. Telling the teacher or principal when kids bother you is a good way to:
    a. Get lots of friends.
    b. Get respect of other kids.
    c. Make kids hate you.
    d. Look mature.

20. Telling on other kids is a good idea when:
    a. They make fun of you.
    b. They have injured someone or are about to injure someone.
    c. They point their middle finger at you.
    d. Insult your mother.

21. If you hurt me, you will respect me most when I:
    a. Tell you that you hurt me.
    b. Tell the teacher that you hurt me.
    c. Tell your parents that you hurt me.
    d. Tell my parents that you hurt me.

22. When you get mad at people for hurting you, they are most likely to:
    a. Apologize for hurting you.
    b. Want to buy you a present.
    c. Get mad back at you.
    d. Think you are cool.

23. Most bullies:
    a. Are heartless demons.
    b. Want to send people to the hospital.
    c. Like to kill defenseless animals.
    d. Would feel bad if they actually broke someone's bones.

24. When you stop getting mad at bullies, they:
    a. Will immediately thank you for being so nice.
    b. Will treat you worse for the first couple of days.
    c. Will immediately think you have changed.
    d. Will immediately feel sorry for having bothered you.

25. To stop being a victim of bullies, you have to refuse to get mad at them:
    a. 50% of the time.
    b. 25% of the time.
    c. 100% of the time.
    d. 90% of the time.

26. If you always follow the advice in this book:
    a. You will never, ever be bullied again.
    b. You will be bullied every day.
    c. People will hate you.
    d. You will still get picked on once in a while.

Section Three: Some Good Advice

Don't Be a Sore Loser

Wouldn't it be great if you could always be a winner in life? Unfortunately, it's impossible. Earlier in the book, I explained that life is like a game. Sometimes you win and sometimes you lose. No one wins all the time. The good news is that if you understand the advice in this chapter, you'll be a winner even when you lose.

Winning feels good and losing feels bad. That's how it has to be. Mother Nature made us that way because she wants us to be as successful as possible. But no matter how terrific we are, there are going to be people who are smarter, stronger, better looking, richer and more successful than we are. We have to learn to live with losing even though losing isn't fun. In fact, it is more important to learn how to deal with losing than with winning. Anyone can handle winning; it feels good. Losing is the hard part.

It is not only in games or sports that we can be losers. We can lose in all types of life situations. We can feel like losers when other kids get higher test scores, when our parents don't give us what we want, when other people win prizes, and when kids tease or bully us and make us look like fools.

Many kids are only happy when they win, and act as if the world is coming to an end when they lose. They scream or argue or cry. This is called being a sore loser. Do you ever act like this? Well, it doesn't make anyone like or respect you more. You only look like a big baby and others won't want to be your friends or play with you again.

Sore losers like to hold grudges. They are so mad about losing that they can't forget about it or forgive the person who defeated them. They stay angry forever. Anger is like a poison that actually makes you sick. When you hold grudges, you want to be hurting the person who hurt you, but the person you are harming the most is yourself. Holding grudges is like swallowing poison and hoping the other person will get sick.

To be happy, you have to take pleasure in other people's accomplishments.

So how can you stop yourself from being a sore loser? By doing the following:

1. Realize that you can't always be the winner and there is nothing terrible about losing. Games are fun to play even when you lose. Of course winning is better, but you can't have the opportunity of winning if you don't also have the chance of losing.

2. Understand that no one is going to hate you if you lose. Do you hate people who lose against you? Of course not. It makes you happy that they lost and you won. Well, the same thing is true about others. In fact, people are more likely to be upset if you defeat them, so don't worry how they'll feel about you if you lose. If you are playing on a team, it is possible that your teammates will be mad at you if you play lousy and cause them to lose. But as long as you do your best and stay calm about your errors, they won't stay mad at you for long.

3. Congratulate your opponents when they defeat you. This is called "being a good sport," and is the opposite of being a sore loser. Even when you lose, you will come out a winner. People will respect you and like you for your mature and gracious behavior, and they will be happy to play with you again. Let's say you win against someone else. What would you rather have your opponents do? Go crazy and scream at you, or say, "Wow! You really played great!"? Of course you would rather have them congratulate you, so you should do the same thing if you are the one who lost.

Remember: you should use these rules not only when you are playing games and sports, but even when you are playing the game of life. If bullies get the better of you, admire them for their success. This way you will feel better more quickly, and you will gain the respect of your bullies. Do your best to come out a winner next time, but don't be sore at them just because they won.

Getting Revenge

You have been suffering day after day, maybe for years, because of the cruelty of other kids. The more pain you have felt, the more you have wanted revenge. You have probably spent a lot of time imagining ways to get back at those who have caused you misery. You may have dreamed up ways of torturing them or making them look like the biggest idiots in history. You want to make them regret they ever even thought of picking on you. You would like them to be so afraid that they will never, ever disrespect you again.

Perhaps you have seen movies like *Revenge of the Nerds*. While there are many movies about victims of bullying who turn the tables on their tormentors and make them suffer, life rarely has the kind of happy endings you see in the movies. In real life, the nerds seldom succeed in carrying out clever plots to humiliate their tormentors. If you cunningly attempt to get back at them, chances are you'll come out looking like an even bigger fool.

Sometimes victims do actually carry out their desire for revenge. Sadly, they often do things that are much, much worse than whatever their bullies did to them. That is because they try to get back in one instant for all the suffering they have been enduring for months or years. If you were to succeed in getting the kind of revenge you sometimes imagine in your mind, you would probably end up in very serious trouble and may also feel terrible for what you did.

So what should you do with your desire for revenge? First, you need to understand the situation correctly:

1. You have to accept the fact that, unless you become a criminal, you will not be able to make your bullies pay for all the pain they have caused you.

2. You want to be a winner, but every moment you spend thinking about revenge you are being a loser. Instead of enjoying yourself, you are wasting your life on angry thoughts about your bullies. This means they are defeating you. They are continuing to control your thoughts without even lifting a finger, and you are doing their work for them!

3. Remember that your bullies are not completely to blame for what they did to you. As you learned earlier, by getting mad at your bullies and trying to stop them, you were actually making their behavior continue — just like the boy throwing breadcrumbs to the pigeons. Is it really fair to make them suffer when you were practically begging them to torment you? It's like throwing bread to pigeons and then shooting them for the crime of eating the crumbs. Furthermore, if you have been telling on them to teachers, principals or parents, you have given them a good reason to want to hurt you. From their point of view, they have been *your* victims.

Now that you understand this, these are the things you should do:

1. Live by The Golden Rule, "Treat others as you would like to be treated." When you seek revenge, you try to treat others as badly — or even worse — than they have been treating you. Then they will want to get back at you even more, so the war will intensify. The Golden Rule says you should be kind to your bullies even when they are mean to you. When you treat them like friends instead of enemies, they will become friendlier, and you won't have any need to get revenge.

2. The best way to get revenge is to turn your tormenters from winners into losers. By following the advice in this book, your bullies will feel like fools whenever they try to bother you. They will be shocked and disappointed to find they can no longer beat you. While this may not be as gratifying to you as seeing them carried off in an ambulance, it is a much healthier solution for both you and them.

Not only will the need for revenge disappear, you will also have the satisfaction of feeling your bullies respect you. You may even discover that kids who once used to make fun of you are now trying to become your friends! Ceasing to be the victim and changing your life is the best possible revenge.

Apologize

Wouldn't you just love it if your bullies were to apologize to you for being mean? If they were sincere about it, would you continue to stay angry at them? Not likely. You would probably feel tremendous relief. Your anger would go away, and you would be glad to be their friends. Even though you may feel your bullies deserve to be seriously punished for having made you suffer, you would let them get away without punishment in return for a few words of sincere regret. That is the amazing power of an apology.

Do you have bullies who are mad at you? As you learned earlier, such bullies are not *true* bullies. When people are angry, they feel like victims. So the bullies that are angry at you probably believe that you are the bully and they are the victims.

Whenever two people are angry at each other, they would each like the other to apologize. However, weeks, months, or years can go by and no one apologizes. They are afraid that if they apologize, they are admitting that they are wrong and they come out the loser. So the state of war continues and they both make each other suffer.

But this is the wrong way to think. When you apologize, you don't lose anything. You come out the winner. And the other side also wins because the conflict ends for them, too, and you make them feel better.

Apologizing is a wonderful thing not only because it makes the other person feel better, it makes *us* feel better, too. Having someone mad at us can make us miserable, especially when the person is important to us. It may even make it hard to enjoy life and to concentrate on other matters. When we apologize, it is like getting rid of a big burden and we feel happier and lighter.

Apologizing means that you let others know that you are sorry for having hurt them. It doesn't necessarily mean you're wrong about everything you said or did, only that you regret having done something that hurt them. When you apologize to people, do you think it makes them more upset with you? Do they think, *"Oh, so you admit you hurt me! I'm going to get back at you for that!"* Of course not. They are relieved to hear that you recognize the way you made them feel, and they may even admire you for having the courage to apologize. Then they are likely to forgive you. And once you admit that you treated *them* badly, it becomes easier for them to admit that they haven't been treating *you* so well, either.

You may wonder why you should apologize to your bullies. After all, they are the ones picking on you, not the other way around.

If they aren't angry at you, then you shouldn't apologize. But if they are angry, it means they feel like they're your victims. So ask yourself: *"Do I give the bullies dirty looks? Do I pray they get hit by a train? Do I tell on them? Do I call them names or hit them back? Do I threaten to get my big brother to beat them up? Do I tell other people how mean they are?"* Even though you feel justified, these are not nice things to do. They are contrary to The Golden Rule. Your bullies feel entitled to be mad at you and to make you suffer. Once the cycle of anger gets started, it doesn't matter who started the conflict.

If you are doing any of these things, getting your bullies to stop bothering you is probably a simple matter: Apologize.

First, ask the bullies if they are mad at you. They will probably say "Yes." Then ask them sincerely if you have done anything to hurt them. If they tell you what you have done, apologize for it. Tell them you didn't intend to hurt them and assure them you will not do it again. And say it like you mean it. Don't try to justify yourself.

Your pride may tell you they should apologize to you first, especially if they started the conflict or have been hurting you much more than you've been hurting them. But don't let that get in the way. If you sit around waiting for them to apologize before you apologize, you may wait forever.

Make your apology unconditional. That means you shouldn't say, *"I'll admit* I *was wrong if you admit* you *were wrong."* No one wants to get this kind of apology. Apologize regardless of whether the bully has any intention of returning an apology.

If you apologize and the person accepts it, that's great. If not, at least you'll feel good knowing you did the right thing.

The Smart Way to Say "No"

Throughout life, people ask us to give them things or do things for them. It is impossible to do everything people ask of us. Furthermore, if we always try to give them what they want, they don't appreciate it. Instead, they take for granted that we have to give them whatever they want, and just get mad at us when we have to turn them down.

If someone asks you for something and you say "No," they may get mad at you. They may feel you are mean and don't want to make them happy. They think you are acting like an enemy. They may try harder to convince you to give them what they want, or even threaten to hurt you if you don't.

Here is a simple way to say "No," so that no one gets mad at you or gives you a hard time:

"I wish I could give it to you (or do it for you), but I can't." Then add the reason why.

Once you say, "I wish I could," people can't be mad at you for not *wanting* to make them happy. They can't feel you are acting like an enemy because your heart is on their side. As long as you're not hurting anyone, it doesn't even matter if your reason isn't true. If you can't think of a good reason why you're unable to fulfill the request, simply say "I wish I could, but I can't," without further explanation. Remember, you don't owe everyone everything they ask of you.

You should do this with your parents, too. If they ask you to do something but you can't at the moment, don't get mad. Just say you wish you could do it now. Calmly explain why you can't, and tell them when you *will* be able to. Or if it's something you can't do at all, explain why. You'll probably find that they respect you for your mature manner and won't bug you.

Keep Your Sense of Humor

This may sound like a strange instruction. You may be thinking, *"What does keeping my sense of humor have to do with being picked on?"*

Kids become victims of constant teasing when they lose their sense of humor about themselves.

Do you like to laugh? Do you like jokes, humor and comedy? Of course you do. You may watch hours of comedy on television every week. You probably like to hear jokes and tell jokes. I bet you like to read funny books.

You may also have heard the expression, "Laughter is the best medicine." And it's true. Laughter helps us get better when we're sick. It helps people survive the harshest ordeals in life. Without laughter, life would be way too serious and we would all be miserable.

Consider what we laugh about. Do we laugh when people look smart? Do we laugh when they are brave or wise? Do we laugh when they are generous or strong? Do we laugh when good things happen to them?

No! We laugh when they look stupid or clumsy or miserable. We laugh when bad things happen to them. You may not have been aware of this till now, but start paying attention to the jokes and comedy routines that make you laugh. Try to think of a joke that doesn't put anyone down (riddles don't count; that's a different kind of humor). I don't think you'll be able to do it. You will quickly realize that when you laugh, someone is being made fun of.

That's what a sense of humor is all about. It is about enjoying people's weaknesses. And it's not a bad thing — it's a good thing! That's why laughing feels so good and helps us heal.

We have to be able to laugh at ourselves when we look like fools.

There are two sides to a sense of humor. One side is being able to laugh at other people. This is the easy side. Whenever we laugh at jokes, at comedy shows, or at people acting stupid or clumsy, we are exercising the ability to laugh at others. Few of us have any difficulty with this.

The other side of humor is the difficult side. What is the other side? Let me ask you, if we're going to laugh at other people when *they* are looking stupid or clumsy or miserable, who are *other* people going to laugh at? The answer, of course, is *us*. There is no such thing as a life in which only *other* people look bad. Sometimes *we* look bad, too, and others are going to want to laugh at us. And that's why the other side of humor is so important: we have to be able to laugh at ourselves.

Think about it: What is an emotionally healthy person? Is it someone who takes himself so seriously that he gets mad whenever someone makes fun of him? No. It's someone who knows he's not perfect, can take a joke about himself and make a joke about himself.

No one is perfect. We all have faults and imperfections that can be laughed at. The truth is that we see each others' imperfections better than we see our own. If I have a big nose, you don't see it? If I'm fat, you don't notice? Of course you do. You see these things better than I do. Do I really need you to make believe you don't see them?

You guys are so ugly, when you look in the mirror the reflection throws up!

We all have the choice to get mad or to laugh when people make fun of our imperfections. If we get mad, it is because we believe others should treat us like we are perfect. This belief is a trap — it is the opposite of a sense of humor. When we believe we have a right to be treated like we're perfect, all someone has to do is suggest that we are *not* perfect, and then we go nuts. And when we go nuts, we *really* look like fools. However, if we realize that it's okay to have imperfections and to laugh about them, then we don't turn into losers. When we can laugh at ourselves and let others laugh at us, people like us and respect us more. And we can like and respect ourselves more, too, when we get rid of the idea that we have to be perfect.

Pay attention to comedies on TV. You will see that the characters are always making fun of each other, and they hardly ever get mad about it. They are showing us the right way to handle putdowns. Life becomes a lot more enjoyable when we can laugh at each other and at ourselves. Chances are, if you have a good friend, you make fun of each other sometimes and neither one of you gets upset about it.

Are you thinking that it's hard to have a sense of humor about yourself? Truth is, your ability to laugh at yourself is right inside of you. Laughter and humor are basic human traits. People all over the world laugh and tell jokes, and they've been doing it forever. It's programmed into our genes. That's why kids start laughing at funny sounds and faces when they are babies. Did your parents or teachers have to teach you what's funny and when to laugh? No! You knew it all by yourself because Mother Nature made us that way.

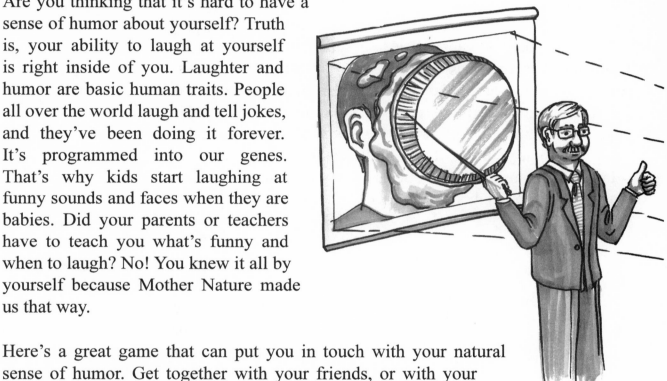

Mr. Smith gives lesson on humor.

Here's a great game that can put you in touch with your natural sense of humor. Get together with your friends, or with your brothers and sisters, and take turns insulting each other. The rule is that no one is allowed to get angry no matter what the insult is. Anyone getting angry earns a point, and the kid with the most points loses the game. If adults are nearby, make sure to let them know it's a game and that no one is being hurt. You will discover this is great fun. You will be making real honest-to-goodness humor, and you will all laugh your heads off! You will discover you can actually enjoy being made fun of.

You may then decide to make humor a bigger part of your life. Since humor has the potential to offend people, here are a few simple rules to help you avoid trouble:

1. It is always safest to make fun of yourself. No one can claim you hurt their feelings if you made fun of yourself.

2. Make fun of people only when you know they can take it as a joke. If they can't handle it, it's better to keep your comments to yourself. (And maybe you should get them a copy of this book).

3. Never make fun of people when you are angry with them. Then it becomes a hostile attack, and they will feel offended and get mad back at you.

_____ Is that your face or a zit with teeth?

Don't worry that people will lose respect for you if you make fun of yourself. Just the opposite is true. They will love you for making them laugh and will respect you for having the courage to make fun of yourself. And when they see you are able to laugh at yourself, it will be easier for them to laugh at themselves, too. Before you know it, you'll be able to laugh at each other.

Never make fun of people
when you are angry.

1. People can be happy:
    a. Only when they win all the time.
    b. Only when they lose all the time.
    c. Even when they lose.
    d. Only when they are better than everyone else.

2. Holding on to grudges is like:
    a. Eating ice cream and hoping your friend will enjoy the taste.
    b. Swallowing poison and hoping the person you are mad at will get sick.
    c. Playing basketball and hoping the other team wins.
    d. Giving money to charity and hoping poor people benefit.

3. If you lose a game, the following is the best way to treat the winners:
    a. Congratulate them for playing so well.
    b. Stick out your tongue at them.
    c. Refuse to play with them again.
    d. Agree to play with them again only if they promise to let you win next time.

4. If you actually succeeded in carrying out revenge plans against people who tormented you, you are likely to:
    a. Win everyone's admiration.
    b. Make them feel like fools.
    c. Get in trouble and feel terrible for what you did.
    d. Scare them so much they will never want to bother you ever again.

5. If you apologize to people for hurting them, they are most likely to:
    a. Think you are a wimp and a loser.
    b. Become madder at you for admitting you hurt them.
    c. Want to hurt you.
    d. Admire your courage and forgive you.

6. Apologizing to someone who is mad at you will probably:
    a. Make both you and the other person feel better.
    b. Make both you and the other person feel worse.
    c. Make it harder for both of you to concentrate on other matters.
    d. Make you feel like you have placed a heavy burden on your shoulders.

7. Apologizing to others means:
    a. Admitting you were wrong about everything.
    b. Pretending you are sorry for what you did.

    c. Admitting you were wrong if they admit they were wrong.

    d. Regretting having hurt them.

8. When people ask you for things:

    a. You should never give them what they want.

    b. You should always give them what they want.

    c. You can't always give them what they want.

    d. You should get mad at them.

9. Which is the smart way to say "No" when someone asks you for something?

    a. Yell, "Stop asking me for things."

    b. Say impatiently, "Go ask your parents."

    c. Say sarcastically, "Do I look like Santa Claus?"

    d. Say sincerely, "I wish I could give it to you, but I can't."

10. We laugh when:

    a. People look stupid, clumsy, and miserable.

    b. People look smart, happy, and talented.

    c. People look rich, pretty, and generous.

    d. People look brave, powerful, and influential.

11. Emotionally healthy people:

    a. Take themselves so seriously that they get upset whenever anyone criticizes or pokes fun at them.

    b. Can laugh at other people but not at themselves.

    c. Believe they are perfect.

    d. Know they are not perfect and can laugh at themselves.

12. It's okay to make fun of other people only when:

    a. You know it will hurt them.

    b. You are angry at them.

    c. You think they can handle it.

    d. Other people are around to laugh at your joke.

13. If you make jokes about yourself:

    a. People will lose respect for you.

    b. You will get in trouble.

    c. No one will laugh.

    d. People will admire you for your courage and find it easier to make jokes about themselves, too.

Section Four: Specific Situations

How to Handle Insults

Insulting Stereotypes

How to Handle Insults about Disabilities

When Kids Insult Your Clothing

How to Handle Rumors

Physical Attacks

When Kids Chase You

When Kids Take Your Things

When Kids Exclude You from Their Group

When Kids Ask You to Choose Between Friends

Bullying Over the Internet

When Siblings are Bullies

Parents as Bullies

Teachers as Bullies

When Other Kids Are Bullied

Section Four Quiz

How to Handle Insults

The single most common way that kids bully each other is by name-calling. It probably happens ten times as often as any other type of bullying. Even most physical fights begin with insults. People call you or your mother bad names, you get mad and tell them to stop, they challenge you to make them, and before you know it fists are flying.

Until now, you've been thinking, *"Oh, no. They're making fun of me. I have to make them stop."* That's the wrong way to think. As long as you think you have to make them stop, they are never going to stop. The real reason they've been insulting you is *because* you have wanted them to stop.

The solution is very simple: It's called "Freedom of Speech"! The United States Constitution, in the First Amendment of the Bill of Rights, gives people freedom of speech. So does every democratic country. It's like the Constitutional version of the slogan, *"Sticks and stones can break my bones but words will never harm me."* Freedom of speech means that people have the right to say whatever they want, as long as the words don't directly cause physical harm (like yelling "Fire!" in a crowded movie theater, or ordering people to commit crimes).

If you believe that people *don't* have the right to insult you, you are denying them freedom of speech. Get rid of this belief. It's a trap. If you believe kids don't have a right to insult you, all they have to do is insult you and then you get mad. Since they love it when you get mad, they'll never stop insulting you.

How would you like it if people got mad at you and tried to get you punished every time you said something *they* didn't like? You'd hate it. So if you want the right to say whatever *you* want without being punished, then you have to give *everyone else* the same right. You should feel fortunate to live in a country where you and I have the right to say what we want without being punished.

From now on you're going to tell yourself, *"If kids want to make fun of me, it's perfectly okay. They can do it all day long and it doesn't bother me in the least."* If kids make fun of you and you don't care, who's going to look stupid, you or them? They will. And who will feel stupid? They will. Do you mind if they look and feel stupid when they call you names? Of course not. You'll be happy. So from now on, when kids insult you, you are going to be happy. You will be the winner, they will feel stupid, and it will require no effort.

If you have been doing the Verbal Bullying Experiment, you should already know what it is like. If you haven't been doing it, now is a great time to start.

There are all kinds of ways you can respond in real life situations, but they should all follow two basic rules: 1) Don't get upset; 2) Do nothing to make them stop.

If kids call you names during class, you should completely ignore them. You are there to learn, and you can get in trouble if the teacher hears you talking. Don't worry that kids will consider you rude if you don't answer them. They aren't stupid. They know perfectly well that students aren't supposed to be having conversations in class. They are the ones being rude, not you, and they know it.

Nerd! Geek! Idiot! Fatso!

Come on gimme something to work with here!

If the teasing happens outside of class, you need to judge if ignoring is the right way to go. If kids are calling names to you from a distance, or if they are saying things about you to each other, I would recommend not doing anything at all. Simply continue minding your own business.

However, don't walk away just so that you won't have to hear them. This will show them their behavior is bothering you, and it should be clear to them that it isn't. They may also feel tempted to follow you if you walk away. Walk away only if you need to be somewhere else.

If kids insult you to your face, ignore them only if you are sure they won't get mad. Ignoring can be considered rude and the teasers may get angry. They may even want to hit you to see if they can provoke you to anger. Of course, they are initiating the rudeness, but that doesn't matter. You want to avoid traps. Your goal is to make people like you, and rudeness in return won't work.

It can be very satisfying to give teasers a taste of their own medicine by responding with an even more clever insult that will make them look and feel like fools. Then they won't want to risk insulting you again. This is okay as long as you really aren't angry when you insult them back. However, I am not going to encourage this for two reasons: 1) You have to be quick-thinking and self-assured to pull this off well. You may not have this ability. 2) It may not get them to like you better. They may look for other opportunities to get back at you.

There are two approaches I do recommend. Both of these are easy since you can memorize the responses.

The first approach is to use the rule of treating whatever people say as the words of your best friends. Thank them for what they say and invite them to do it all they want. The following responses can be used with just about any insult:

1. Thank you for noticing.

2. It's so nice of you to care about me.

3. If you like to make fun of me, be my guest.

4. If it gives you pleasure to put me down, you can do it all day long.

5. Please tell me more.

6. Any time you feel the urge to make fun of someone, please come to me.

The second approach is to use humor. This is more powerful and in most cases will make the teasers immediately like you and respect you. But I only recommend making jokes about yourself because that is safer than making fun of the teasers. The basic idea is that you agree with the insult, and insult yourself even more than they did. Here are some samples:

Teaser: You are so ugly.

You: If you think *I'm* ugly, you should see my *mother*!

Teaser: You look gross.

You: I know. Whenever I look in the mirror, the *reflection* throws up.

Teaser: You are such a geek.

You: I hope so, I've been training since birth.

Teaser: You are a real idiot.

You: Yes. Back in the old country, my ancestors were the *village* idiots.

Teaser: Your mom is a fat pig.

You: If you think my *mother's* fat, you should see my *grand*mother!

The teasers do not expect you to answer in this way. You will catch them off guard, and there's a good chance they'll respond with a real, honest laugh. They will think you are cool and like you for it. These kind of responses work because they immediately let the teasers know they have no power over you, you're a good sport, you're not afraid of them, you aren't defensive, and you don't attack. It is practically impossible for someone to feel like your enemy after you answer with jokes about yourself.

You may think that it is all right not to get upset only if the teasing is lighthearted. But what if it is mean-spirited, meaning that the teasers really intend to hurt your feelings? Shouldn't you get upset? Shouldn't you tell on them? Shouldn't they be punished?

The answer is "No!" It doesn't matter how the teasers feel when they are insulting you. They still have freedom of speech. It is your response that determines how the situation will turn out. If the teasers insult you in a lighthearted way but you get mad at them and try to make them stop, they will *become* angry and mean-spirited. On the other hand, if they start out mean-spirited but you answer with humor, then they will laugh and *become* lighthearted.

Remember, the worst thing you can do is tell on the bullies. The only time to tell is if they have caused a true injury or to prevent them from injuring someone. You should never, ever tell on someone for calling you names. There is nothing wimpier than telling a teacher or principal on a kid for saying a bad word to you. It doesn't matter if the insult was said in front of a whole bunch of students. If the insult itself made you look like a fool, telling will make you look like an even bigger fool.

Insulting Stereotypes

It's easy to upset people with insulting stereotypes about their race, religion, gender or sexual orientation. Today, these insults are considered especially offensive. It's easier for you to get others in trouble if they make fun of your group than if they make personal insults about you. (But don't do it.)

The belief that insulting the group you belong to is worse than personal insults leaves you vulnerable to attack. If kids discover they can't upset you by calling you idiot or ugly but they can get you angry by insulting your group, then that's what they will do.

If people would be blind to group differences, every group would be treated the same and there would be no group stereotypes. However, it is impossible to overlook our differences. We are biologically programmed to notice them. Do you think you could

look at a group of tourists from another continent and *not* notice they are different from you? Not likely. People from other groups will notice *your* group differences as well and will form stereotypes. What should you do when people insult you with stereotypes about your group?

Unfortunately, many fights break out because people are sensitive about their group and treat those who insult them as enemies. But the truth is that handling insults about your group is no different from handling insults about your body or intelligence. If you make the mistake of getting mad about the group insults, people will continue insulting you and will lose respect for you *and* your group. If you don't get angry, they will stop insulting you. And you will gain respect for yourself and your group.

There is nothing especially terrible about people noticing your group differences and making remarks about them, as long as they don't commit any crimes against members of your group. Unfortunately, people have a tendency to paint other groups as being worse in some way and create negative stereotypes about them. Spreading negative stereotypes encourages hatred and can lead to bloody conflicts.

If you are concerned about negative stereotypes that others have of your group, the best way to stop the stereotyping is by letting them get to know you as an individual. Then they will see that all groups are basically the same despite the superficial differences. If you stay angry with others because they stereotype you, you treat them like enemies and turn them away from you. They'll only get to see you as a hostile member of a bizarre group. Therefore you have to treat them like friends even when they are being insensitive.

Use the rules for turning bullies into buddies and this won't be hard to do. Strange as it may seem, you should give people freedom of speech even for negative stereotypes. If you believe that people *do* have a right to stereotype you, then you'll have no reason to be angry with them when they do it, so the stereotypes will have no power over you. Treat the stereotypes as the words of your best friend. Show gratitude for the valuable information they are bringing. Of course, you don't have to accept what they are saying as true, only that they are intending to help you.

I'll show you how it works. Let's say my ancestors came from an imaginary country called Gerbalia. We Gerbalians have green skin and big noses. Most adult Gerbalians have high paying jobs and many people think we are stingy. Now a White kid is making fun of me. First, the wrong way to handle it.

White kid: Hey, Izzy, how come Gerbalians are green? I bet you're all covered with snot!

Green kid *(me)*: That's disgusting! You apologize!

White kid: Okay. I'm sorry you're covered with snot!

Green kid: Hey! That's no apology! I mean it! You better stop making fun of Gerbalians!

White kid: I'll make fun of Gerbalians all I want. And you all have such big noses!

Green kid: No we don't! My nose is only a little bit big, and some Gerbalians have noses even smaller than yours!

White kid: Not on this planet! And you Gerbalians are so cheap. You only buy things on sale.

Green kid: That is a dirty lie. You better shut your mouth already, you racist!

White kid: Yeah? How are you going to make me? By getting your rich relatives to sue me?

Green kid: Not all Gerbalians are rich!

White kid: You can't fool me. You Gerbalians are always cheating the rest of us and stuffing your bank accounts!

Green kid: We don't cheat people! Shut up already! I'm reporting you to the principal, you big fat bigot!

My efforts are only leading me to Losersville. Am I making the White kid stop with the insults? No. Respect me? No. Like me? No. Get rid of his stereotypes about Gerbalians? No. Am I treating him like a friend or an enemy? An enemy, of course. I am getting angry with him, defending my group, threatening and attacking him. All these things will make him remain my enemy.

Now I will show how to treat him as a good friend and use humor to make him like me.

White kid: Hey, Izzy, how come Gerbalians are green? I bet you're all covered with snot!

Green kid: You're right! Let's shake hands!

White kid: Ugh! And you Gerbalians have such big noses.

Me: Do you want to know why our noses are so big?

White kid: Yes.

Green kid: Because air is free!

White kid: Ha! And why are Gerbalians so cheap? You only buy on sale.

Green kid: You know why God created White people?

White kid: No.

Green kid: Because *someone* has to pay full price.

White kid: Ha! Tell me, how come you Gerbalians have so much money?

Green kid: Because we value education and try to get important jobs that pay well.

White kid: So education is the secret?

Green kid: Yes. If you get a good education, maybe my uncle will hire you.

White kid: You know, for a Greenie, you're all right!

Green kid: Thanks. For a Whitey, you're not so bad yourself.

The results were much better this time. I didn't work any harder than the other time. In fact, it was much easier. I was completely relaxed and my blood pressure didn't go up. I simply used the rules for treating people like friends. I told myself that everything he says, no matter how nasty, is because he cares about me. I didn't defend myself or the Gerbalians. I didn't attack him or fear him. My jokes about my own green Gerbalian group made him laugh, and then he could let me joke about White people without getting mad at me. I quickly got him to like me and respect me. And he realized that maybe Gerbalians aren't so horrible after all.

How to Handle Insults about Disabilities

What if you have disabilities that make you stick out like a sore thumb? Perhaps you use a wheelchair, or have vision or hearing problems, or you have a learning disability or some medical condition that makes you look or act different. You notice that people stare at you more than you like, and some kids make fun of your differences. How should you handle it?

What's the matter, four-eyes? Never seen a thumb before?

Your discomfort over being singled out is easy to understand. It is upsetting that life was so unfair to you. If only something could be done to forbid people from noticing your differences.

Human beings, as well as other species, are programmed to notice things that are different from usual. This ability helps us survive. It also means that we are naturally curious about people who are different from us and have a strong urge to look at them.

Until now, you have probably been telling yourself, *"They have no right to look at me as though I'm some kind of freak!"* If you think this way, you will become mad whenever someone pays you too much attention. The first thing you need is to realize that people *do* have the right to look at you all they want. There are no laws against staring, so there's no reason to be mad at them for doing it.

The second thing is to accept that life is not fair. Even if life were absolutely fair, we wouldn't be happy. We would be terribly bored because we'd all be exactly the same.

Once you accept that life is not fair, you free yourself from bitterness and become lighter and more carefree. Fate may have dealt you a bad hand, but don't judge by appearances. You may think others are luckier than you because they don't have your problem, but you never know what problems they have that you can't see. Kids can appear physically perfect and seem to be leading rich full lives, yet feel even more miserable than you. Life contains hardships. If you triumph over your difficulties, you become happier and stronger.

My last suggestion is to use your sense of humor when kids make fun of you. It's healthier to laugh about your hardships than to get upset about them. You might say something like, "If you want to look for more than five seconds, I have to charge admission." Or "My condition is contagious. You catch it by looking." And don't forget the line, "If you think *I'm* strange, you should see my *mother* (or father, sister, etc)!" As long as people enjoy being with you, your unusual traits won't be all they see.

When Kids Insult Your Clothing

Many arguments erupt over insults about the clothes people wear. For most people, the way they dress is important because it determines the way they are perceived by others. This is especially true for kids. When fashions change, kids rush to buy the new styles and hate to be caught wearing something that is no longer "cool."

Insults about clothing can be a great way to get kids upset. If this is a problem in your life, it doesn't have to be. There are two things you can do to stop insults about your clothes: 1) Change your attitude about clothing. 2) Change the way you respond to insults about your clothing.

People judge you not only by the way you dress. Your personality is far more important than your clothing. The better people get to know you, the less important clothing becomes. You can have the coolest clothing in the world, but if you are nasty to people, they will have a lousy opinion of you. On the other hand, if you wear out-of-date hand-me-downs but are funny, interesting and kind, people will think good things about you.

If you enjoy dressing attractively and you can afford it, that's fine. However, if you believe it is important to wear cool clothing so that people will like you, you are giving them power over you. Don't think that spending

Hurry! Mustn't be seen in last season's clothing!

SALE→

lots of money on the latest styles and hottest brand names will make anyone like or respect you more. The sooner you stop worrying about how you look, the sooner you become a winner.

Now, what do you do if other kids make fun of your clothing? The following is an example of how you might fall into a trap:

Cool dresser: I can't believe what nerdy sneakers you have.

You: They're not nerdy!

Cool dresser: Yes they are. Where did you buy them? Kmart?

You: It's none of your business where I buy my shoes. And they are not nerdy!

Cool dresser: They sure are. Your parents are too poor to buy you good sneakers.

You: No they're not! And stop talking about my parents!

Cool dresser: I'll talk about your parents all I want.

By defending your shoes and your parents, you automatically lose. You are treating the kid as an enemy and acting like a sore loser, unable to accept that your clothing is not as cool as the other kid's.

However, you will become a winner if you treat others like best friends and compliment them for having better clothing:

Cool dresser: I can't believe what nerdy sneakers you have.

You: Yeah, they are kind of nerdy. I love the way *you* dress. It's so cool.

Cool dresser: Oh, thank you. If you want, I can tell you where I shop.

You: Sure. Thanks.

This time you turned a kid who was insulting you into a friend. The amazing thing is that you didn't lose respect by acknowledging that your clothing is nerdy. The kid enjoyed your compliment, and now likes you and wants to help you. Of course, if you don't really care about where other kids shop, you don't have to make believe you do. As long as you compliment them on their clothing and don't defend yourself, they will like you and respect you. And they will stop insulting your clothing.

How to Handle Rumors

It can be quite upsetting when people spread rumors about you behind your back, or if they tell you they heard rumors about you. The following conversation between Rob and Cindy is a typical example of how it happens:

Cindy: I heard you wet the bed last night.

Rob: No I didn't!

Cindy: But that's what everyone is saying.

Rob: Who is saying it?

Cindy: Jason. He slept over at your house and he says you did it.

Rob: He's a liar! I didn't wet the bed!

Cindy: Why would he say it if it weren't true?

Rob: I don't know. And I don't believe he would say it. He's my friend.

Cindy: He did say it, and he's telling everyone.

Rob: I'm going to ask him, and if he says you're lying, you're going to pay!

Cindy: Are you threatening me?

Rob: Not really. But you better stop saying I wet the bed.

Cindy: But everyone is saying it. And everyone knows it's true.

Rob: It is not true! You better not believe it!

Cindy: Why shouldn't I believe it? Jason was at your house. He wouldn't lie.

Rob: It is not true! I haven't wet the bed since I was eight!

Cindy: Ha! I know you still wet the bed!

Rob is clearly losing. He's getting nowhere in stopping Cindy from talking about the rumor or believing that it's true.

What is *really* going on here? Cindy is playing a game with Rob. She gets him to fall into a trap by taking advantage of the instinct of defense. She brings him a nasty rumor, and it horrifies Rob. He doesn't want anyone saying it, so he argues that it's not true. He wants to win, but by defending himself he automatically loses. And the harder he tries to make the rumor stop, the more he looks and feels like a loser.

So what should you do if people bring you a rumor? Don't be duped into the trap of defending yourself. Win the game by turning the tables on the rumor-bringers. Make them defend *them*selves. How? By using the following four-word question: *"Do you believe it?"* There are only two ways to answer: Yes or No. Here's what happens if Cindy says "No":

Cindy: I heard you wet the bed last night.

Rob: Do you believe it?

Cindy: Uhhh...no.

Rob: Good.

And that's the end of that. Cindy has nothing more to say about the rumor. She feels foolish for having brought him the rumor and lets it drop.

Here's what happens if she answers "Yes":

Cindy: I heard you wet the bed at night.

Rob: Do you believe it?

Cindy: Yes.

Rob: You can believe it if you like.

And that's usually where it ends. Cindy gets stuck with nothing smart to say. If she keeps asking if it's true, Rob should only let her know that she has the right to believe it if she wishes. If Cindy wants to believe a stupid rumor, what does that make her? Stupid, of course. And this should be perfectly fine with Rob.

What if the rumor is true? What should you do then?

It makes no difference. The reason they bring you the rumor has nothing to do with the truth; the purpose is to make you the loser. You are not required to admit it's true if you don't want to. So whether the rumors are true or not, just calmly ask "Do you believe it?" If they answer "No," you say "Good," and if they answer "Yes," you say "You can believe it if you want."

There is one possible exception to this rule. Let's say someone who really cares about you asks you about a rumor. Tell them the truth only once and don't get into a long discussion. If they say they don't believe you, do not defend yourself. Just say, "You can believe it if you wish."

If you overhear others spreading rumors about you, what should you do?

Nothing! As with insults, the freedom-of-speech rule applies. If you try to deny others the right to say the rumor, they will show you that you can't stop them. If you get angry and defensive, kids will wonder why it bothers you so much and will be more likely to believe it's true. So don't get upset. Don't try to find out who started the rumor. Remember, everyone has the right to say whatever they want. When they see you truly don't care about the rumors, they will have no fun spreading them and will stop.

If a friend informs you that a rumor is being spread about you, handle it like Rob:

Cindy: Everyone is saying you wet the bed last night.

Rob: Really?

Cindy: Yes! Aren't you going to do anything about it?

Rob: No.

Cindy: Aren't you worried people are going to believe it?

Rob: No.

Cindy: You mean you're just going to let people spread rumors about you?

Rob: Sure, if they want to. It's their right.

This way you easily come out the winner and earn people's respect.

Physical Attacks

WARNING: *This advice applies only with bullies who are basically emotionally stable. There is a tiny percentage of kids that are extremely disturbed and dangerous. If they are threatening you, you should either avoid them or make sure you have people to protect you when you are near them.*

Serious fights don't just happen out of nowhere. Almost every physical fight starts with a word fight. Kids call you names. You tell them to shut up. They tell you to make them, and in a flash fists start flying. However, if you follow the advice in this book, words will never make you mad and physical fights won't erupt.

Some adults may tell you not to let anyone get away with hitting you. They believe kids should always fight back, and that the only way to stop being bullied is to stand up for yourself and beat up the bully. Here's what you should know about this advice.

1. Sometimes fighting back ends the problem, but it usually doesn't, so you can't rely on it. The same kids get into fights again and again. These fights happen *because* the kids fight back.

2. Fighting back is dangerous. You may get seriously hurt and, instead of winning, become a big loser. The bully is going to love getting you to fight again so he can beat you up some more. If you win, the danger isn't over. The bully will be on the lookout for an opportunity to attack you when you are vulnerable, or he may get his friends to beat you up.

3. Fighting can get you punished by your school, so even if you win the fight, you are a loser. And if you injure the other kid, you will probably get into *really* serious trouble. If you lose the fight, you may still get punished for simply being involved, so you come out being a double loser.

Karate, schmarate. You dare lay a hand on me and my parents are gonna sue!

If parents or others have been encouraging you to fight and you are afraid to disobey them, don't worry. Just try the advice in this book for one week and you should see the problem improve dramatically. Then your parents won't have to continue telling you to fight back because no one will be bothering you anymore.

Rather than hitting back, use everything you've learned in this book about turning bullies into buddies. Treat them as though they are your best friends. Remember, odds are they don't really mean to injure you. Bullies just want to get you mad and in trouble, and you can keep that from happening.

I coulda sworn this used to bother her...

This is what to do if kids hit or push you and you are not hurt. Just act as though nothing happened. You know they only want *you* to get in trouble, so they probably will not risk attacking you again, or will just do it very lightly. Again, don't respond. Don't tell on them, because then they'll know they succeeded in bothering you. Plus, they'll be mad at you for telling on them and will try to get back at you later. If you don't respond, not only won't they have the pleasure of annoying you, they also won't have any reason to be mad at you. Other kids will think you are tough and mature — not a crybaby. You will gain respect.

If a kid really does hurt you, should you ignore that, too? No! No one has the right to hurt you. But before you decide what to do, determine if you need medical help or not. If another kid hits you or pushes you hard, chances are you don't have bones broken or need stitches. If you are in pain, just show you are hurt. Do not get mad. In a calm but serious voice, say to the attacker something like, "That really hurt. Please be careful." It is much better to talk to your attackers by yourself than to tell an adult. This increases the chances that they'll apologize, and your pain will soon go away.

What if they keep on hitting you hard even though you're telling them it hurts? Ask them why they are hitting you. If they stop long enough to answer, then you may be able to save the situation and turn it into a useful conversation. Remember to treat them like good friends. If they have a good reason for being mad at you, let them know you understand and offer an apology.

You: Why are you hitting me?

Bully: Because I hate you.

You: Did I do something to hurt you?

Bully: Duh! You keep telling the teacher on me.

You: I guess that wasn't a very nice thing to do. I'm sorry.

Bully: Well, you better not do it again.

You: Okay. From now on, if I have a problem with you, I'll talk to *you*.

Of course, it might not work out quite this nicely. They may not have a good reason for hitting you. Maybe they'll say they just don't like your looks or your background. If they stop long enough to let you talk, you still may be able to make things better by using humor and the rules for turning bullies into friends.

You: Why are you hurting me?

Bully: Because I hate nerds.

You: I don't blame you.

Bully: How can you say that? You *are* a nerd.

You: Do you think I would be a nerd if I had a choice? I'd much rather be cool like you.

Bully: Really?

You: Sure. But I don't like it when you hurt me.

Bully: Sorry. I didn't mean to hurt you.

If the attackers don't give you a chance for conversation, give them this warning: "I really don't want to see you get in trouble." This lets them know you'd prefer to be on their side rather than against them, and that the choice is theirs. If they are smart, they will stop hitting you. However, if they continue, you must do your best to avoid injury. Get away from them if you can. If you can't, yell for help. If there is no help around, then hit back if it is your only choice. In self-defense, the law allows you to do whatever is necessary to prevent yourself from being seriously harmed.

What do you do once the fight is over? If you aren't injured, find an opportunity to talk to the kids like friends. It may be necessary to ask your teacher or school counselor to arrange the meeting. Then ask the kids why they attack you. If it turns into a real discussion, great! Let them know you aren't looking to get them in trouble, but that they really hurt you and you would like them not to do it again. However, if they still insist on hurting you, they deserve to be reported to the authorities.

If the bully not only caused you pain but actually injured you, you *must* let the authorities know. Injuring people is more than just bullying; it is a serious crime. No one has the right to injure you. Whoever does should be made to pay for their crime so they learn not to do it again. However, still try to see them as a friend. If you are given a chance to confront your attackers, let them know your goal is not revenge but to teach them that they can't get away with crime. Help them understand that if they continue to behave this way toward people, they may eventually end up in jail, and that would be a real shame.

When Kids Chase You

You are in the schoolyard or on your way home, and kids start chasing you. They've chased you before and you always run away because you're afraid of them. Or maybe you just find them annoying. You wish they'd stop.

What's the solution? All you have to do is stop running away! The truth is, without realizing it, you have actually been encouraging others to chase you by running away from them.

You can test this out with a little experiment using a brother, sister or friend. Ask them to chase you. Then run away. You will discover they keep chasing you as long as you run away. After a while, stop running and say, "I give up."

Now ask them to chase you again. This time just stand there. You will discover that they don't go anywhere, either. It is impossible to chase you if you aren't running away.

It's impossible to chase someone who isn't running away.

Don't follow this advice if the people chasing you really want to hurt you. Standing there will only make it easier for them. If you truly believe they are chasing you because they want to harm you, running away may be the best thing to do. Get help if necessary. However, unless you have given the kids a really good reason to hate you — like by telling on them and getting them in trouble — your fear of being hurt may be exaggerated. They're probably just trying to have fun by seeing how afraid you are.

Instead of running away from people as though they are your enemies, tell yourself that everyone is your friend. This way you won't be scared and need to run away. Kids will like and respect you more when you stop fleeing from them.

When Kids Take Your Things

Bullies often demand you give them your possessions or forcefully take them from you. What should you do about this?

The slogan, "Just Say No," doesn't apply here. If kids ask you for something, like money or your lunch, and you just say "No," you may be giving them a good reason to be mad at you by refusing to make them happy. So you should always treat them like friends. Never get mad when people ask you for things. Remember the smart way to say "No." Respond with, "I wish I could…but I can't," and give a reason. Here are some examples:

Mom, can you make me five more lunches? I need them so Bobby, Frankie, Evon, Tyler and Dustin will stay my friends.

Bully: Give me your lunch.

You: I wish I could, but I need it.

Bully: Hey, I'm really hungry.

You: I can tell. So am I. I really wish I had an extra lunch to give you.

Bully: Let me copy from you during the test.

You: I wish I could, but I can't afford to get in trouble.

or:

I wish I could, but cheating is against my principles.

Bully: Give me your money.

You: I wish I could, but I can't. I need it for school supplies.

If someone asks to borrow money, you can answer like this:

Bully: Lend me a dollar.

You: I wish I could, but I'm not allowed to lend money.

If someone borrowed money from you once before and never returned it, and then asks for another loan:

Bully: Lend me a dollar.

You: I wish I could, but you haven't returned the last dollar I lent you.

There is a chance the bullies may threaten to beat you up if you don't give them what they want. Don't be scared, and answer like this:

I wish I could give you my grandmother's wheelchair, but my parents would never forgive me.

Bully: Give me your money.

You: I wish I could, but I need it.

Bully: I'll beat you up after school if you don't give it to me.

You: I'm sure you could if you wanted to.

Bully: So give me your money.

You: I would love to, but I can't.

The bullies are not likely to beat you up, especially if you talk to them in this respectful manner. Bullies, no matter how big they are, are rarely looking to hurt you. They just want to scare you. So don't fall into the trap.

If a bully continues to pester you, continue saying that you'd love to give him what he wants, but you can't, until he gets worn out and leaves you alone. He probably won't come to you again asking for things.

The following is a terrific way to respond when a really tough bully asks you for something you could afford to give away:

Bully: Give me your sandwich!

You: It would be an *honor* to give you my sandwich!

And give it to him graciously. This will catch the bully off guard and may immediately turn him into a buddy. He was expecting you to act terrified and sheepishly wriggle out of the predicament. Instead, you confidently and elegantly filled his request. You will have earned his respect and appreciation. Don't be surprised if he declines the gift and tells you he was just testing you. You will have passed with flying colors.

What if kids take something from you by force? It's important to realize they usually don't really intend to keep it. They are just playing a game with you and trying to get you upset. So the worst thing you can do is get mad. It's also a bad idea to try to grab it back. The best thing to do is remain calm. Wait patiently and they will probably give it back. And the calmer you are, the quicker they'll return it.

However, if they don't return your belongings even though you are remaining calm, they should not get away with it. This is stealing, and society protects you from such crimes. But don't get mad and hurry to tell on them. Calmly say something like, "I really *do* need my hat back." If they don't return it by the time you need it, you can say, "I would like my hat back, and I really don't want to get you in trouble." If they don't get the message and return the hat, then report it to the appropriate adults. If the object was taken by schoolmates, tell the school. If neighborhood kids took it, tell their parents or your own parents.

When Kids Exclude You from Their Group

It can be painful to be excluded from a group, or a *clique*, as it is sometimes called. If it happens to you, you may find yourself feeling like unwanted garbage, not good enough for them. Exclusion is a favorite tactic of girls, but boys can do it just as well.

What can you do about it?

If you get upset when kids exclude you, they have defeated you. They feel good while you feel like a loser. Then they *continue* excluding you because who wants a loser as a member of their group?

The secret to handling exclusion is not caring if kids do it to you. Then it can't have power over you.

"How can I just not care?" you may be wondering. It hurts to be rejected by a whole group.

The way to stop caring is by realizing it is the way to win and become more popular. If kids see you as a loser, they will want to exclude you. If they see you as a winner, they will want to include you. If you want to win, don't give the group power over you and don't care about being excluded.

You will discover a strange fact: The less you care about being accepted, the more the group will want you to join.

When kids exclude you, it makes you feel like they are evil. But they aren't. If you think of them as evil, you are giving them a good reason to want to exclude you. Why shouldn't they exclude someone who thinks of them so terribly?

But if they aren't evil, why are they excluding you? It's because everyone wants friends, and everyone wants to feel special. But it is only possible to be close friends with a small number of people. Exclusive cliques enable kids to have close relationships and feel special at the same time. Adults do it, too. They form cliques at work, and they join various groups and organizations.

I changed my mind. You can join us.

The less you care about belonging, the more people will want you to join.

Isn't it neat that the teacher said you have to be my friend?

You may wish that adults would force kids to include you in their groups. But apply The Golden Rule and you'll realize it's not a good idea. Ask yourself, *"Would I like to be forced to be friends with kids I didn't choose?"* Of course not. In fact, you might go out of your way to be *un*friendly to them. So if you don't want to be forced to be someone else's friend, you shouldn't want other kids to be forced to be your friend. Imagine the teacher instructing the class to stop excluding you and start being your friends. Do you really think anyone is going to respect you more? Will your classmates think, *"Wow, you're so cool. I wish the teacher would help me get friends, too."* Not likely. Maybe a couple of nice kids will make an effort to be friendly to you. For most of the kids, though, the teacher will have just made it more obvious that you are a big loser with no friends.

Accept that it is perfectly okay for kids to leave you out, and that no one has to be your friend if they don't want to. Then you will walk around with a smile instead of a frown. Smiles attract people, while frowns repel. When you are no longer afraid of being excluded, it will become much easier for kids to want to befriend you.

Be ready to be friends with whoever is ready to treat you as a friend. You will find that as long as you are happy with yourself, there will be kids who are happy to be with you. If the really popular group won't include you, so what? The members of the "in" group aren't necessarily any happier than kids who are part of a more "nerdy" group. It's the quality of friendship that counts, not how cool the members act or dress.

When Kids Ask You to Choose Between Friends

If a friend asks you to stop being friendly with someone she is mad at or doesn't like, your friend wants you to show loyalty by treating that person like your enemy, too. This puts you in an uncomfortable position. You would like to continue being friends with both of them, not lose one friendship for the sake of the other. What should you do?

First of all, it is rude to pressure you to choose between friends. Your friend will be happy if you become the enemy of her enemy, but this won't make your friend like or respect you more. In fact, you will get *less* respect for acting like a puppet. The best thing is to respect your friend's right not to be friends with the other person, but don't allow her to dictate who *your* friends will be.

If you truly love me, you'll be mad at Allison, too.

Tamara: I want you to stop talking to Brittany.

You: Why?

Tamara: Because she's a geek.

You: If *you* don't want to talk to her, you don't have to.

The matter may end there. However, Tamara might not let you off the hook that easily. She may insist that you stop talking to Brittany. But stand firm. Don't let her dictate your friendships.

Tamara: I want you to stop talking to Brittany.

You: Why?

Tamara: Because she's a real dork.

You: If you don't want to talk to her, you don't have to.

Tamara: And I don't want *you* to talk to her, either.

You: But she didn't do anything wrong to me.

Tamara: Well, she did something wrong to me, and if you are my true friend, you won't talk to her.

You: I *am* your true friend. And if you don't want to be Brittany's friend, that's definitely your right.

Tamara: But if I see you speak to Brittany again, you are not my friend anymore.

You: I will always consider you my friend. But if you don't want to be my friend anymore, I can't stop you.

Don't worry about picking between friendships. If you handle it this way, there's little chance you will lose your friends. They will respect you for standing up for your principles, and won't want to lose you as a friend. They might be mad at you for a little while, but as long as you don't get mad back, your friends will stay your friends for a long time.

Bullying Over the Internet

The same principles apply to bullying over the Internet as bullying face-to-face.

The Internet is amazing. You can get information from all over the world on any subject in a matter of seconds. You can spread information just as quickly. The thing that makes the Internet so wonderful is also what makes it so dangerous. People can spread information or lies to whomever they want.

They can also take things you write and pass them on to others. If you write something nasty about someone and send it to a friend, your friend can then send copies of it to his friends. Before long, lots of people know what you said about that person, including the person himself. So be very careful about what you write. It is probably a good idea not to write bad things about anyone. If you don't like others spreading nastiness about you, you shouldn't do it to them, either. You are much safer making nice comments than mean or critical ones. This is true in life as well.

But don't get mad if something negative is said about you over the Web. Don't write angry emails or carry out investigations to see who started the rumors. You will look like a fool and people will enjoy keeping the rumors flying. Stay calm. Let others know you can't stop them from saying what they want online, and that it's perfectly okay if they spread nasty rumors about you. This will take away a lot of their fun, and you will look tough and gain respect.

If people ask you if what they read about you online is true, handle it just like any other rumor. Ask them, "Do you believe it?" If they say "No," you say, "Good." If they say "Yes," respond with "You can believe it if you wish." Then you always come out the winner.

And you can use humor. Instead of simply telling people they can believe the rumor if they want, you can say an exaggerated version of the rumor is true. For instance, if kids write that you do drugs and someone asks you about it, you can say your whole family does drugs together every night, including your goldfish and parakeet. Since this will sound ridiculous to them, they won't believe the part about your using drugs, either. If you don't take the rumor seriously, neither will others.

When Siblings are Bullies

If your family is like most families, you and your siblings fight just about every day. Maybe even all day long. Most adults think sibling rivalry is normal. Some even believe brothers and sisters are born wanting to hurt each other, and that it's a parent's job to protect them. Truth is, siblings are born loving each other. If you observe wild animals that are biologically similar to humans, like chimpanzees, gorillas and orangutans, you will see that siblings get along very well. Older ones help take care of the younger ones. Watch a brood of puppies or kittens and you will notice that they play together beautifully all day long. Your brothers and sisters will get along nicely with you, too, if you follow the instructions in this book.

Tell me quick. Where's my sister Jessica?

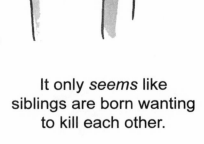

Until now, your siblings have been telling on you and trying to get you in trouble with your parents. And you have been doing the same to them. If you want to be friends with your siblings, here is the first step: Stop telling on them!

It only *seems* like siblings are born wanting to kill each other.

Does this sound like crazy advice? Well, it's not. You will discover that when you stop telling on your siblings, they will soon stop telling on you. They will feel like jerks if they tell on someone who never tells on them.

No matter how annoying they are and how often they tell on you, say to yourself: *My siblings have the right to tell on me all they want, but I will not tell on them.* If they bother you, don't get mad. Just tell them (nicely) that you don't like what they are doing. Remember, the only time to tell on people is when they do something truly terrible, or to prevent them from doing something truly terrible.

Any disagreement can turn into a fight over mom.

It may be very difficult, but even if your siblings lie or make up stories about how you hurt them, don't defend yourself and don't get mad. If your parents believe the lies and punish you, don't get mad at *them*, either. Don't argue or yell at them for blaming you unjustly. Just take the punishment like a hero.

Why? Because it's going to make you the real winner! First of all, your siblings will be totally blown away by you. They'll be amazed that you are so nice to them and so strong that you can gracefully accept punishment for something you didn't do. But they will also feel guilty. They know they lied and you didn't really deserve what they did to you.

If your parents hear your siblings bothering or making fun of you, they may get mad at your siblings and want to punish them, even though you aren't upset. Let your parents know there is no problem and you can deal with your brother or sister yourself. Say to them, *"It's okay. We're just fooling around,"* or something like that.

Don't worry, Mom. We're only fooling around.

Make a point of defending your siblings from your parents, and your siblings will be grateful and keep you from getting in trouble. Your parents will be overjoyed when they see such loyalty. There is nothing that makes parents happier than seeing their children stick up for each other, even if it is against them.

Parents as Bullies

Do your parents boss you around? Do they yell at you, blame you and punish you if you don't act like a robot completely under their control? Are you dreaming of the day when you can leave the house and live on your own? You are not alone. Many children in families feel this way.

You may believe it's impossible to get your parents to treat you differently. But if you follow these instructions, and don't expect your parents to give you absolutely everything you want, your parents will do much more for you than they are doing now, and you will all be happier.

It may seem to you that your parents want you to be perfect. But what your parents really want from you is *respect.* It is more important to them than anything else. Even if you are as perfect as a kid can be, they will not be happy with you if you don't show them respect. On the other hand, if you have many faults and don't always do what your parents ask of you, they will still like you and treat you well as long as you show them respect.

You may be asking yourself, *"Why should I give my parents respect if they are making me miserable — yelling and screaming and going nuts on me all the time."* The reason? Show them respect and they will *stop* yelling and bossing you around. Once you start treating them with respect, they will show you respect in return.

Another reason? They *deserve* your respect. Even though they may seem like your worst enemies, they love you more than anyone else in the world. They do more for you, too. Yet who do you take for granted more than anyone in the world? Probably your parents. You know you can disobey them and they will still give you food, clothing and everything else you need.

If you were to speak to your friends the way you speak to your parents, you probably wouldn't *have* many friends. If you yelled at your teachers the way you yell at your parents, do you think you'd be able to remain in class very long? You'd be spending lots of time in the principal's office instead. And if you disrespected the principal the way you disrespect your parents, you'd probably be sent to a psychiatrist!

It may seem to you that your parents are trying to boss you around. But do you do more for your parents or do they do more for you? They cook and clean and shop and do your laundry and drive you around and go to work so they can make enough money to pay for all the things you need. The truth is, *you* are *their* boss. *They* are working for *you*! If they are mad at you, it is only because they feel you are treating them unfairly. They slave for you, but whenever they make a request of you, you give them attitude. Can you blame them for being mad?

Because your parents love you so much, you can scream at them, insult them and disobey them, and they will still feed you, clothe you, give you a room to sleep in and provide you with whatever else you need. They act like your servants, so it is very easy to disrespect them.

If your parents are making you miserable, it's because you both are in the trap of getting mad at each other. Anger, as you have learned by now, makes the other person keep on being mean. If you want your parents to stop being mean to you, show them they can't get you mad no matter what they do.

If you find it hard to treat your parents with respect, just think about how you treat your teachers. They make you work hours a day in school, and then you go home and do more work for them. Yet you don't scream, curse or insult them. You treat them

You can have this house rent free. All you have to do is keep it clean.

No way. It ain't worth it.

respectfully. If you can be respectful to your teachers, you can be respectful to your parents, who love you and serve you so much more.

How do you show respect to parents? Treat them like your employer. The amazing thing is that if you treat your parents as though they are your boss, they will actually boss you around *less*! Most often, what your parents want you to do takes practically no time, and you end up doing it anyway. For instance, they ask you to take out the garbage. It takes a couple of minutes. Instead of doing it after they yell at you 10 times, do it the first time they ask. It takes the same couple of minutes, but you save your parents the need to yell at you and you save yourself a headache. You show your parents respect, as well.

They ask you to clean your room. Instead of making their blood pressure hit the ceiling for a week till you get around to doing it, do it right away. It takes the same amount of energy as doing it later, but your parents will be so proud of you. And they deserve to have you clean it. You may call it "your" room, but did you buy it? No. Your parents did. It's really *their* room, and they are nice enough to let you use it. If they want you to keep it clean in exchange for free rent, it's an awfully good deal. So do it. It's worth it.

Do you talk to your parents rudely? With the same amount of effort, you can speak politely and prevent a needless argument over the way you talk.

If they punish you, don't argue and don't get mad. Just take your punishment like a mature person, as though you deserve it, even though you feel you don't. You will find they reduce punishment very quickly when you accept it. Let me show you how it works. First, the wrong way:

Parent: Go to your room! You hit your brother!

Child: No I didn't!

Parent: Don't argue with me! You are always hitting your brother!

Child: You are so unfair! He's not even hurt!

Parent: Stop talking back to me or your punishment will be doubled!

Child: You are so mean! You are always taking *his* side!

Parent: Shut your mouth and go to your room already!

This approach can only lead to bigger trouble. Now here is a better way to handle it.

Parent: Go to your room! You hit your brother!

Child *(In a polite, concerned voice)*: You think I hit my brother?

Parent: Yes.

Child: Is he hurt?

Parent: I don't think so.

Child: Good. Would you like me to go to my room?

Parent: Yes.

(Child quietly goes to room.)

If you handle it this way, I bet your parent will quickly give you permission to leave your room.

Even if your parents forbid you from doing what you want, tell yourself they act this way because they love and care about you. Show that you respect them and they will give you more freedom. Let's say you want them to let you go to a movie late at night. First, the wrong way to handle it:

Child: I'd like to go to the movies at ten o'clock tonight with my friends.

Parent: You can't go so late.

Child: Why not?!

Parent: Because I said so! It's too late for someone your age.

Child: But all my friends are going!

Parent: That's not my business. I said you can't go and that's it!

Child: You're so mean! You treat me like a baby!

Parent: I'm not mean! And stop arguing with me!

Here's the better way to handle it:

Child: I'd like to go to the movies at ten o'clock tonight with my friends.

Parent: You can't go so late.

Child: Are you worried about me?

Parent: Yes. I think ten o'clock is too late for someone your age to go to the movies with friends.

Child: I really appreciate your concern for me, but I think you can trust me to stay out of trouble.

Parent: Yes, you have been acting kind of mature lately. Let me think about it.

There's no guarantee you'll get *everything* you want from your parents by behaving respectfully, but I guarantee you'll get much more than you will by being angry and rude. When you yell and argue, you sound like a baby, which proves to your parents you can't be trusted. But when you treat them with respect, they see you are mature. And you will be amazed how much freedom and responsibility they will be willing to give you.

Teachers as Bullies

Are your teachers mean to you? Do they treat you worse than they treat other kids in class? Are you the one they blame whenever there is a problem? Are they dissatisfied with your work, no matter how hard you try? Does it seem like they would love to see you fail? And are you so mad at them that you wish they'd get hit by a truck?

If you're mad at teachers because they pick on you, I'd like to tell you a secret. The reason they pick on you is *because* you are mad at them. When you are angry, you treat them like the enemy. Don't expect them to treat you nicely in return.

Teachers really do care about you and want you to do well. They like to see kids learning; then they feel they are doing a good job. They are happier to give you high marks than a lousy report card. But teaching is difficult and teachers are responsible for many children all day long. If you give them a hard time by complaining or fighting them, they will not appreciate having you in their class. If you make them miserable, they will not feel encouraged to make you happy.

Teachers deserve respect, and if you give it to them, they will like you and do their best to teach you. Think of them as your friends in school, and that's how they will treat you. Instead of getting mad at them if they treat you unfairly, remind yourself they care about you and feel good about themselves when you succeed. It's possible they simply made a mistake. So don't be mad at them. No one, even you, is perfect.

I just *LOVE* to flunk my students.

Let's say you get a test back and you feel the mark was lower than you deserved. Here is the wrong way to handle your teacher:

Student *(crumpling up test paper and throwing it in garbage)*: I hate you, teacher!

Teacher: What are you doing?

Student: I'm throwing away the stinking test! You're so unfair!

Teacher: What are you talking about?

Student: You marked me wrong and everybody else right!

Teacher: Show me where.

Student: The test's in the garbage.

Teacher: So get it out and show me.

Student: *You* get it out of the garbage!

Teacher: You threw it in the garbage, not me. If you want me to look at your test, *you* get it out!

Student: I'm not getting that rotten test out of the garbage where it belongs!

Teacher: Well, maybe it's time for you to take a stroll to the principal's office and tell her your story.

You see, nothing good is likely to come from treating the teacher like an enemy. Now let's consider how it can turn out when the teacher is treated like a good friend:

Student: Teacher, I'd like to talk to you about my test score.

Teacher: Sure.

Student: I'd like you to look at a few of my answers. I'm not sure, but I think you may have made some mistakes in scoring them.

Teacher: I'd be happy to take a look. If you can show me that I made a mistake, I'd be glad to raise your mark.

Student: Thanks a lot.

It's always to your advantage to treat your teachers with respect. You will be amazed at how much more they will do for you if you stop thinking of them as people who are out to get you.

When Other Kids Are Bullied

You have reached the final chapter of this book. You now know what to do when *you* are bullied. But what should you do if you see other kids being picked on?

Helping others is not a simple matter. You may have been told by teachers or other school staff to stand up for kids who are being bullied. Sometimes, though, we make things worse by getting in the middle of other people's fights. These are some of the things that can happen:

1. The bullies may become mad at you for taking another kid's side against them. They may decide it's okay to get some of their friends to help, too. So you may end up with extra enemies and put yourself in unnecessary danger.

2. The bullies will probably get angrier at the victim, too, for getting you to take sides against them.

3. As you understand by now, kids who get picked on a lot are not really such innocent victims. Without realizing it, they are encouraging the bullies to continue picking on them. If you take their side against their bullies, you will be giving the victims the (wrong) impression that they are the "good guys" and the bullies are the "bad guys."

4. You'll get in the way of the victims learning how to handle their own problems. The only people in the world who can make the bullying stop are the victims themselves. If you stand up for them, they will learn to expect others to come to their rescue whenever anyone bothers them.

This is how it might turn out if you take the victim's side against the bully:

You *(to bully)*: Hey, leave that kid alone!

Bully: Who do you think you are?

You: It doesn't matter. You have no right to bully anyone!

Bully: Says who?

You: Says me!

Bully: Are you going to stop me?

You: If I have to!

Bully: Just try! I'll beat both of you up!

You: You're not allowed to threaten people. I'm going to tell the principal on you!

Bully: Oh, big baby! You are going to *tell*.

As you can see, this approach can get you involved in the fight. The victim may like you for helping, but the bully is going to hate you. You may get yourself beat up, too, especially if the bully is a better fighter than you.

So what *should* you do when you see someone being bullied? The general rule is that you should put yourself on the *bully's* side and help the victim at the same time. You don't want to take sides against the bully, especially if the bully is stronger than you.

If the bully is merely insulting the victim, there is a very effective way to help: by using humor. Join the bully in insulting the victim, and then you insult yourself, too. Here is how it works:

Bully *(to Victim)*: You are a big fat idiot!

Victim: No I'm not!

Bully: Yes you are!

You *(to Victim)*: You *are* a big fat idiot! And so am I!

This will probably make both the victim and the bully laugh. And the victim will realize that if you can make fun of yourself, he shouldn't get upset about insults, either.

If the victim is being attacked physically, the situation is more dangerous, so you have to use your judgment. If you are stronger than the bully and he is afraid of you, tell him something like, "I'm sorry, but I can't let you beat up my friend." Say it calmly but firmly, without being angry. This should be enough to stop the fight.

If the bully is not afraid of you, then you have to be especially careful. As with the insults, you may be able to help by taking the bully's side while helping the victim:

You *(to Bully)*: Boy, he must have really hurt you!

Bully: No, that wimp can't hurt me.

You: So how come you want to beat him up?

Bully: He's just a geek. He can't even take a joke.

You: Yeah, I know. But I'd hate to see him get hurt. Let me talk to him and I'll see if I can stop him from getting mad so easily.

Bully: Good. He could really use that.

You: Thanks for letting him go.

Bully: No sweat. He's lucky to have a friend like you.

It may not always turn out this well, but it is certainly better and safer than trying to act like a hero rescuing victims from evil villains. Of course, if the situation is very serious and you are not able to stop the fight on your own, go for help.

Once the incident is over, try to help the victims learn how to solve their problem. Explain to them that bullies bother them because it's fun to see them get mad. Teach them that if they stop getting upset, the bullies will eventually leave them alone. And, of course, you can recommend that they read this book.

1. The most common way that kids bully others is by:
   a. Hitting.
   b. Stealing.
   c. Name-calling.
   d. Spreading rumors.

2. The Constitutional solution to becoming a victim of teasing is:
   a. The right to vote.
   b. The right to assemble.
   c. Freedom of speech.
   d. The Declaration of Independence.

3. Freedom of speech is the Constitutional version of the slogan:
   a. A rolling stone gathers no moss.
   b. A bird in the hand is worth two in the bush.
   c. He who lives in glass houses shouldn't throw stones.
   d. Sticks and stones may break my bones but words will never harm me.

4. Freedom of speech means:
   a. People have a right to say whatever they want, as long as it doesn't directly cause physical harm.
   b. People have a right to say whatever they want as long as it is nice.
   c. People have a right to criticize the government but not individual citizens.
   d. The President can make a speech on television whenever he wants.

5. If kids call you names during class, you should:
   a. Tell the teacher right away.
   b. Completely ignore them.
   c. Write down what they said and tell the teacher after class.
   d. Have your parents write a note about it to the principal.

6. Jimmy calls Nakeisha a fatso. Nakeisha says, "If you think I'm fat, you should see my mother!" Jimmy is most likely to:
   a. Hit her.
   b. Think she is crazy.
   c. Call her father a fatso, too.
   d. Laugh and think she's funny.

7. If people make nasty remarks about your race or religion, you should:
    a. Report them to the police.
    b. Treat it like any other insult.
    c. Say an even worse insult about their race or religion.
    d. Tell them what they're saying isn't true.

8. If you have a disability that is very noticeable, you should:
    a. Tell people they have no right to stare at you.
    b. Hide so that no one can make fun of you.
    c. Wish that people who look at you get hit by a speeding car.
    d. Give people the right to look at you all they want.

9. To be happy, you should:
    a. Believe that life doesn't always have to be fair.
    b. Go to the county fair once a year.
    c. Dye your hair a fair color (blonde is best).
    d. Insist that life always be fair.

10. If you don't wear the latest fashions:
    a. No one will want to be your friend.
    b. Everyone will laugh at you.
    c. No one else really cares.
    d. Don't even *think* of leaving the house.

11. If people spread rumors about you, you should:
    a. Tell everyone the rumors are lies.
    b. Let them.
    c. Spread rumors about them.
    d. Believe them.

12. If someone asks you if a rumor they heard about you is true, you should:
    a. Find out who started the rumor and beat them up.
    b. Say, "If you believe it, you are not my friend anymore!"
    c. Scream.
    d. Ask them, "Do you believe it?"

13. If someone hits you and it doesn't hurt, you should:
    a. Report the incident to an adult.
    b. Say, "You have no right to put your hands on me."
    c. Make believe you didn't notice.
    d. Tell him to apologize.

14. If someone punches you and it hurts, but you are not injured, you should:
  a. Maturely tell him that it hurts.
  b. Get him in trouble.
  c. Hit him back even harder.
  d. Cry.

15. If you want kids to stop chasing you, you should:
  a. Run away as fast as you can.
  b. Extend your leg to trip them.
  c. Throw rocks at them.
  d. Just stand in one place.

16. Someone takes your pencil without permission. What is the best way to get your pencil back?
  a. Yell, "Hey! Give me back my pencil!"
  b. Tell the teacher that the kid is a thief.
  c. Calmly say to the kid, "I really need my pencil."
  d. Beat the kid up after school.

17. If you want to be accepted by a clique, the best thing to do is:
  a. Ask the school counselor to tell them to let you join.
  b. Not care if they don't accept you.
  c. Start a clique of your own to make them jealous.
  d. Tell them, "I'll do anything you say if you let me join."

18. If kids exclude you from their group, it is because:
  a. They are evil.
  b. They are stupid.
  c. You are evil.
  d. They want to feel special.

19. Kids who belong to a "cool" group:
  a. Are happier than kids who belong to a "nerdy" group.
  b. Are sadder than kids who belong to a "nerdy" group.
  c. Are not necessarily happier than anyone else.
  d. Are a bunch of jerks.

20. Your friend tells you to stop being friends with Alexa. You should say:
    a. "You don't have to be friends with Alexa if you don't want to."
    b. "Don't tell me who my friends should be!"
    c. "Alexa must be a real creep!"
    d. "I promise I'll never talk to her again."

21. If kids write nasty stuff about you over the Internet, you should:
    a. Write nasty stuff about them.
    b. Ignore it and only write nice things about other people.
    c. Tell the school principal.
    d. Send them a virus.

22. You hit your sister and your father grounds you for a week. You yell, "You're so unfair!" and slam the door when you go into your room. Which is probably true?
    a. Your father will say, "I'm sorry, I didn't mean to get you mad. Forget the punishment."
    b. Your father wants to be fair, so he will ground your sister, too.
    c. Your father will feel like grounding you for two weeks because you were rude and slammed the door.
    d. Your father loves your sister more than he loves you.

23. Your brother tells Mom that you hit him. Mom tells you to go to your room for the rest of the day. What is the best way to get the punishment taken away?
    a. Punch a hole in the wall.
    b. Be polite and respectful, and go quietly to your room.
    c. Tell Dad, "Mom is so mean to me. Tell her to let me out of my room."
    d. Tell Mom "I'm not going to do any homework until you let me out of my room!"

24. If you want your siblings to stop telling on you, you should:
    a. Stop telling on them.
    b. Tell on them twice as much as they tell on you.
    c. Tell them, "If you don't stop telling on me, I'm going to beat your brains out!"
    d. Tell your parents that your siblings are liars.

25. If your parents want to punish your brother for bothering you, you should:
    a. Tell your parents, "Thanks. He's always bothering me."
    b. Stick out your tongue at him.
    c. Tell your brother politely, "That ought to be a lesson for you."
    d. Tell your parents, "It's alright. We were just fooling around."

26. If you want your parents to treat you well, you should:
  a. Throw tantrums when they don't give you what you want.
  b. Tell them that they are much meaner than your friends' parents.
  c. Show them respect even when they punish you.
  d. Tell them you hate them.

27. You should respect your parents because:
  a. They deserve respect for all they do for you.
  b. It is a good way to get them to buy you things.
  c. Otherwise you will get punished.
  d. You want them to like you better than they like your siblings.

28. If your parents ask you to do something, you should:
  a. Make them ask you twenty times before you do it.
  b. Tell them to ask your brother or sister to do it.
  c. Tell them to stop bossing you around.
  d. Do it as soon as possible.

29. Teachers are happiest when:
  a. They give their students failing grades.
  b. Their students do well.
  c. Their students get left back so they can teach them another year.
  d. Their students get suspended.

30. If teachers are mean to you, it is probably because:
  a. They hate you.
  b. Their teachers treated them badly when they were kids.
  c. You are disrespectful to them.
  d. They didn't have time to eat breakfast.

31. When you see a bully calling another kid an idiot, the best thing to do is:
  a. Tell the bully that name-calling isn't cool.
  b. Call the bully an idiot.
  c. Hit the bully.
  d. Tell the victim, "You *are* an idiot. And so am *I*!"

About the Author

Izzy Kalman, a school psychologist and psychotherapist living in Staten Island, New York, is an expert in teaching people how to deal with anger and aggression. He is an instructor with Cross Country University, presenting his unique training seminars to mental health professionals throughout the United States. He has been keynote speaker at conferences on children's aggression.

Izzy has developed unique role-playing procedures that produce almost immediate improvement in relationship problems. His Staten Island Community TV series, **Help, They're Driving Me Crazy,** presented his approach to problems in getting along with people.

Izzy's greatest passion is helping children who are victims of relentless teasing and bullying. Following the massacre at Columbine, he created and authored the website **Bullies2Buddies.com** and developed a comprehensive school violence prevention program called **Victim-Proof Your School**. The website teaches kids how to stop being victimized by their peers and instructs parents and teachers how to quickly and easily reduce fighting between children. His lessons for victims are also available as an audio CD program, **How to Stop Being Teased and Bullied Without Really Trying.** Izzy is working on a parenting book on sibling rivalry.

The child of Holocaust survivors, Izzy was born and raised in the Bronx. He earned a Bachelor's degree in psychology from City College in 1974 and a Master's in clinical psychology from Hahnemann University in Philadelphia in 1978. Fulfilling a childhood dream, he then moved to Israel, where he began work as a school psychologist, married a beautiful dark-skinned woman of Yemenite ancestry and had his first two children. In 1988 he moved back to the U.S. with his young family. Their third child was born in 1992.

Izzy can be reached by email at izzy@Bullies2Buddies.com

Does your school need a violence prevention program? There is nothing quite like Izzy Kalman's Bullies to Buddies: Victim-Proof Your School program.

"Every kid should be required to take the Bullies to Buddies course."
— Cindy Fravel, Counselor, Denver, Colorado

"This approach works. For the sake of our students, I hope all educators, parents and teachers will give it a try."
— Jane Steinkamp, Principal, The Jefferson School, Tracy, California

To order additional copies of

Bullies to Buddies
How to Turn Your Enemies into Friends
($15 plus shipping and handling)

Call **1-866-983-1333** or visit **www.BulliestoBuddiesBook.com**
Substantial discounts given for bulk orders

Also available: Izzy Kalman's two-hour audio CD program
How to Stop Being Teased and Bullied without Really Trying
($20 plus shipping and handling)

Seminars, Workshops and Speeches by Izzy Kalman

Does your organization or school need a presentation that is both unique and practical? Izzy Kalman is available for presentations on a variety of topics dealing with relationship problems, anger, and aggression.

"Thank you! This workshop is a true service to humanity."
— *Nancy Butler, Social Worker, New Haven, Connecticut*

"Finally an approach that makes sense. Best training I have ever attended."
— *Carol Banegas, Psychiatric Social Worker, San Diego, California*

"Mr. Kalman's workshop ranks as the best presentation witnessed in my thirty years in the field."
— *David Burton Denson, LCSW*

"This is so simple yet so very amazing. I can't wait to add this to my private practice."
— *Steven F. Winkle, Social Worker, Las Vegas, Nevada*

"Excellent presentation!! Clear, concise techniques for anger control. Everyone should learn this in grade school or before."
— *Elaine Sherwood, Program Director, Bakersfield, California*

For more information on the
Bullies to Buddies: Victim-Proof Your School Program
or Izzy Kalman's services

Call **1-866-983-1333** or visit **www.Bullies2Buddies.com**